My Revision Planner

REVISED

Introduction

About Paper 2

Paper 2 Option 2E.1: Mao's China, 1949–76, is a depth study. Therefore it requires a detailed knowledge of the period that you are studying. Paper 2 tests you against two Assessment Objectives: AO1 and AO2.

AO1 tests your ability to:
- organise and communicate your own knowledge
- analyse and evaluate key features of the past
- make supported judgements
- deal with concepts of cause, consequence, change, continuity, similarity, difference and significance.

On Paper 2, AO1 tasks require you to write an essay from your own knowledge.

AO2 tests your ability to:
- analyse and evaluate source material from the past
- explore the value of source material by considering its historical context.

On Paper 2, the AO2 task requires you to write an essay which analyses two sources which come from the period you have studied.

At A-level, Paper 2 is worth 20 per cent of your qualification. At AS-level, Paper 2 is worth 40 per cent of your qualification. Significantly, your AS grade does not count towards your overall A-level grade. Therefore, you will have to take this paper at A-level in order to get the A-level qualification.

Structure

At AS and A-level, Paper 2 is structured around four key topics which cover the period 1949–76. The AS and A-level exams are divided into two sections. Section A tests your source analysis skills, whereas Section B tests your ability to write an essay from own knowledge. Both sections focus on the four key topics. The question may deal with aspects of one of the topics, or may be set on issues that require knowledge of several or all of the topics.

Aspect of the course	AO	Exam
Key Topic 1: Establishing Communist rule, 1949–57		
Key Topic 2: Agricultural and industrial changes, 1949–65	AO1 and AO2	Section A and Section B
Key Topic 3: The Cultural Revolution and its aftermath, 1966–76		
Key Topic 4: Social and cultural changes, 1949–76		

The exam

At AS and A-level, the Paper 2 exam lasts for 1 hour and 30 minutes. It is divided into two sections, both of which test the depth of your historical knowledge. Section A requires you to answer one compulsory question on two sources. Section B requires you to write one essay. As this is a depth paper, questions can be set on single events or programmes but may cover more extended periods.

How to use this book

This book has been designed to help you to develop the knowledge and skills necessary to succeed in this exam. The book is divided into four sections – one for each of the Key Topics. Each section is made up of a series of topics organised into double-page spreads. On the left-hand page, you will find a summary of the key content you need to learn. Words in bold in the key content are defined in the glossary. On the right-hand page, you will find exam-focused activities. Together, these two strands of the book will take you through the knowledge and skills essential for exam success.

There are three levels of exam-focused activities.
- Band 1 activities are designed to develop the foundational skills needed to pass the exam. These have a green heading and this symbol:
- Band 2 activities are designed to build on the skills developed in Band 1 activities and to help you achieve a C grade. These have an orange heading and this symbol:
- Band 3 activities are designed to enable you to access the highest grades. These have a purple heading and this symbol:

Some of the activities have answers or suggested answers on pages 84–88. These have the following symbol to indicate this:

Each section ends with an exam-style question and sample answers with commentary. This should give you guidance on what is required to achieve the top grades.

1 Establishing Communist rule, 1949–57

China in 1949

Political problems

In October 1949, **Mao Zedong** led his Communist forces to victory in the Chinese Civil War over **Chiang Kai-Shek** and his Nationalists, the **Kuomintang (GMD)**. However, China was backward, lacking an organised central government. There was no history or experience of democratic rule or organised, efficient government. Regions far from Beijing, like Muslim **Xinjiang**, had little in common with the rest of China and places like Tibet did not consider themselves to be Chinese at all.

Chinese society

Social attitudes remained rooted in **Confucian tradition**: women were not considered equal and they did not have the right to own property. Many peasants lived in poverty, exploited by corrupt landlords and threatened by criminal gangs and bandits. Eighty per cent of the population still lived in poor rural areas and survived by farming the land. There was little health care outside of the cities and education was very poor: the vast majority of peasants remained illiterate.

The aftermath of the 1946–49 Civil War

- The war between **Nationalists** and **Communists** had killed millions, destroyed infrastructure and spread poverty and malnutrition.
- Refugees clogged what remained of transport networks and filled the streets of the cities.
- Although the Nationalists had fled to Taiwan, they stripped the country of assets such as gold, silver and dollar reserves, alongside cultural treasures, including those from Beijing's Forbidden City.
- China's economy was completely devastated. There was no stable or even unified currency. However, the biggest problem was **hyperinflation**. Unable to support itself through taxation, the GMD regime had sought to bankroll its armies through printing money. In places, the money economy had collapsed and people reverted to bartering. Shortages of consumer goods led to people hoarding scarce supplies, making the situation worse.
- Many of the educated elite, including bureaucrats and businessmen, had left with the Nationalists. There were few experienced officials left to run cities or with enough technological knowledge to rebuild the economy. The Communist Party did have support in rural areas of the country, where their promises of land reform had appeal, but they were far less popular amongst businessmen and middle classes in large Chinese cities like Shanghai.
- The Nationalists continued to be a threat, bombing ships on the coast to prevent a Communist attack, while killing hundreds in the cities on the mainland. The Nationalists sent spies and saboteurs to attack the new regime.

Complete the paragraph

Below is a sample exam-style question and a paragraph written in answer to this question. The paragraph contains a point and specific examples, but lacks a concluding explanatory link back to the question. Complete the paragraph adding this link.

To what extent is it correct to argue that The Civil War was the main reason for China's problems in 1949?

This statement is correct only to a moderate extent. It is certainly correct to say that the Civil War had a devastating effect on the Chinese people. Industry had been smashed by the Nationalists, who destroyed it rather than let it fall into Communist hands. The Nationalists had funded the war by printing money and this had caused hyperinflation. The Nationalists had been chased off the Chinese mainland but they had fled to Taiwan and taken with them a large amount of China's gold supplies.

Identify an argument

Below is a series of definitions, a sample exam-style question and two sample conclusions. One of the conclusions achieves a high level because it contains an argument. The other achieves a lower level because it contains only description and assertion. Identify which is which. The mark scheme on page 82 will help you.
- Description: a detailed account.
- Assertion: a statement of fact or an opinion that is not supported by a reason.
- Reason: a statement that explains or justifies something.
- Argument: an assertion justified with a reason.

How significant was the impact of the Civil War in weakening the Communists' control of China in 1949?

Sample 1

The Civil War was significant in weakening Communist control of China in 1949 in several ways. Following the war, the Nationalists fled to Taiwan, an island off the coast of the Chinese mainland. Additionally, the economy suffered from hyperinflation. Finally, the Nationalists had destroyed much of China's industry to avoid it being used by the Communists. Therefore, the Civil War was very significant in weakening Communist control of China in 1949.

Sample 2

The impact of the Chinese Civil War was significant in weakening the Communists' control of China because it made it very hard for them to realise the promises that they had made to the Chinese people. However, the impact of the Civil War was not the most important reason why the Communists did not have complete control in China. It is true that the Chinese economy was backward, but this had long been the case: China had failed to keep up with the Western industrial revolution of the nineteenth century. The Chinese nation was made up of many different ethnic groups, languages and traditions. Regions such as Tibet did not consider themselves Chinese at all, while Islamic Xinjiang had little in common with the rest of China. Most people in China were illiterate peasants: they had little idea of what Communist ideology was. The Communists declared themselves in favour of gender equality, but Chinese traditions argued that women were not equal to men. There was little tradition of central government control: bandits roamed the countryside, which was sometimes controlled not by the government, but by warlords and criminal gangs like the Triads. Therefore, while the Civil War was significant in weakening the Communists' control of China, there were significant problems that had existed long before the Civil War and had not been addressed.

The state of China's economy in 1949

The state of China's industry

When the Communists came to power, China's industry had been badly damaged by the years of war and much of China's industrial equipment had been destroyed. In places, retreating Nationalist forces had attempted to sabotage industrial sites to prevent them falling into the hands of the Communists. Areas where local power stations had been bombed or coal stocks were low lacked electricity.

At the end of the Second World War, the **Soviet Union (USSR)** controlled Manchuria in the north-east of China. They dismantled industrial equipment in factories and mines, confiscated tools and gold and shipped them back to the USSR.

Factories needed to be reconstructed before industrial production could be improved. Raw materials were scarce and it was difficult to get them to the factories. In 1949, factory output was 44 per cent below its 1937 level. Furthermore, many skilled personnel who had the knowledge required to rebuild industrial production had fled to Taiwan with the Nationalists.

The state of China's agriculture

The Communists did have support among the Chinese peasants who made up 80 per cent of the population, because they promised to introduce land reform. However, agricultural tools and livestock were in short supply and the most common fertiliser used by the peasants remained human waste. This spread disease. During the Civil War, many peasants had been forcibly **conscripted** into the Nationalist forces to replace soldiers lost in battle to the Communists. The farmers were dragged from their fields. With the farms left unattended, the crops wilted and died. This reduced food supplies to dangerously low levels.

National infrastructure

When the Communists came to power, China was in chaos. The previous Nationalist government had been very corrupt: bribery of officials was commonplace, while many leaders hoarded supplies or sold food meant for the people for their own profit. Transport networks were badly damaged; an estimated half of the railway network had been destroyed. Blowing up railway tracks and bridges had been a key tactic of the Communists during the Civil War because it disrupted the Nationalists' ability to move their troops into battle, but now it created a major problem for the new government. They had to rebuild them quickly in order to consolidate control over large expanses of the country, particularly isolated rural areas far from the capital, Beijing. Telephone lines had been damaged while rivers and harbours were clogged up with ships sunk during the years of conflict.

Mind map

Use the information on the page opposite to add detail to the spider diagram below.

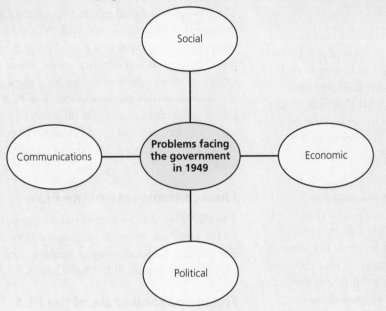

 Spot the mistake

Below is an activity in answer to a question. The factual evidence in the paragraph is correct, but the paragraph can only achieve a mark in Level 2. Read the paragraph and decide why a higher mark cannot be awarded (see page 82 for the mark scheme).

How successful was land reform in winning the support of the Chinese people in 1949?

> The peasants supported the Communist policy of land reform. Land reform made the lives of the Chinese people better. A lot of people in the cities believed that Mao was dedicated to building a 'new' and better China. Land reform increased food production and provided sufficient food for the people in the cities.

The new power structure

The different roles of the Communist Party

The **Chinese Communist Party (CCP)** coordinated the government. Growing to 5.8 million people by the end of 1950, it set economic targets and controlled education and the prison camp system. Important members of the Communist Party held key roles in the government. For example, Peng Dehuai was the minister of defence and also the commander-in-chief of the **People's Liberation Army (PLA)**.

Party **cadres** helped enforce the Party's policies: they controlled schools and the legal system and they monitored the PLA and the civil service, ensuring they remained loyal. The cadres monitored work units called **Danwei**. All employees belonged to one. They controlled permits needed for travel or marriage, access to housing or food. Mass organisations like the All-China Federation of Democratic Youth helped indoctrinate the young, while the All-China Federation of Women mobilised women in support of the regime's campaigns on issues such as birth control and divorce rights.

The government

In September 1949, the Communist Party organised the **Chinese People's Political Consultative Conference (CPPCC)** to meet in Beijing. It appointed the ministers who formed the new government, the Central People's Government. The CPPCC created the **Common Programme**. This was to be a temporary constitution until a full constitution could be written. It set out a range of rights including gender equality, educational opportunity and protection of religious belief. However, it also emphasised the leading role of the CCP, gave powers to the PLA and police to crush opponents of Communism and made Mao the Head of State. The CPPCC acted as the **legislature** while preparing the new constitution.

In reality, the CPPCC did what it was told by the **Politburo**, which was made up of important Communist leaders. The Politburo had 14 members, but the key decisions were made by the five-man standing committee: what they decided became the law. Mao was the chairman of the standing committee, which also included his close colleagues **Zhou Enlai** and **Liu Shaoqi**.

The bureaucracy

The CCP needed a huge number of bureaucrats to help establish the new regime and impose the Party's control over China. A burgeoning bureaucracy was needed to introduce land reform, run the cities and introduce a **centrally planned economy**. The number of state officials increased very rapidly from 720,000 in 1949 to 7.9 million ten years later.

The People's Liberation Army

The PLA played a vital role in helping the CCP establish its control. As Mao famously said, 'All political power grows out of the barrel of a gun.' The PLA was used to round up bandits and criminal gangs. These groups had terrorised many Chinese, so attacking them was a good way of increasing public support. The PLA played a key role in spreading Communist influence. The armed forces attacked Xinjiang and Buddhist Tibet and also chased the remaining GMD out of mainline China: they were forced to flee to Taiwan.

The economic role of the PLA

The PLA played a key part in building popular support for the Communist regime through economic assistance. They rebuilt China's shattered infrastructure: soldiers built bridges, roads, rail links and canals.

The propaganda role of the PLA

During the Korean War, the PLA fought against the combined might of the United Nations (UN). Their struggle gave rise to heroic tales of model soldiers that publicised the values of sacrifice, discipline and commitment to Mao. As many as 800,000 new recruits every year were indoctrinated with Communist propaganda.

Mao's dominant position within the government

The leader of the Communist Party, Mao, also became Head of State in 1949. As the leader who had led the Communists to victory in the Civil War, he held massive personal prestige and influence. It was his ideas, so-called **Mao Zedong Thought**, which became the guiding principles of the new government.

The growth of democratic centralism

The CCP called the new system of government '**democratic centralism**'. It was meant to be democratic because at a local level villages and town councils would elect representatives. These representatives travelled to regional congresses to represent their views. In turn, the regional congresses elected representatives and this process carried on up a hierarchy of organisations until the views of the lowest councils were heard in 'the centre', namely, Beijing. However, at no point was there any chance to vote in favour of a different political party taking power.

! Delete as applicable

Below is a sample exam-style question and a paragraph written in answer to this question. Read the paragraph and decide which option (in bold) is the most appropriate. Delete the least appropriate options and complete the paragraph by justifying your selection.

How far do you agree that the Communist Party had established complete political control in China between 1949 and 1954?

The Communist Party had established political control in China between 1949 and 1954 to a **very great/ moderate/limited** extent. Although the Chinese People's Political Consultative Conference (CPPCC) was the main legislative body and initially included non-Communists, in fact the Communist Party and its Politburo held power. The CPPCC acted as a 'rubber stamp' to the wishes of the Politburo, allowing the Party to introduce its policies. Control of the government meant that the Communists could organise the country to ensure it could **possibly/most likely/definitely** establish complete control of China by splitting it into Bureaux and appointing loyal Communists to key roles running each one. The part played by the PLA was **very great/certainly important/absolutely vital** to the establishment of control because it meant that opposition could be easily crushed. Party cadres enforced Communist policies in schools, factories, the civil service and the legal system. Democratic centralism gave the appearance of democratic representation but there was never any chance for voters to elect a different political party.

! Support or challenge?

Below is a sample exam question which asks how far you agree with a specific statement. Below this is a series of general statements which are relevant to the question. Using your own knowledge and the information on the opposite page, decide whether these statements support or challenge the statement in the question and tick the appropriate box.

'The new government established in the years 1949–54 was essentially a personal dictatorship of Mao Zedong.' How far do you agree with this statement?

Statement	Support	Challenge
Mao was both Head of State and Chairman of the Communist Party.		
The CPPCC included non-Communists.		
Decisions were made by the five-man standing committee of the Politburo.		
Zhou Enlai was head of the State Council.		
Gao Gang, a close friend of Mao, held all four posts in the Manchurian Bureau.		
Peng Dehuai was defence minister and also head of the PLA.		
Mao Zedong Thought was the guiding principal of government.		
Democratic centralism let peasants vote for councils in their villages.		
The Communist Party had 5.8 million members by 1950.		
Party cadres enforced Communist policies in schools, factories and the PLA.		

Defeating the CCP's opponents

The CCP launched the 'Campaign to Suppress Counter-revolutionaries' in March 1950, while the 'Three Antis' campaign (August 1951) and the 'Five Antis' campaign (February 1952) targeted opponents with intimidation, imprisonment and even execution. The campaigns greatly enhanced Mao's control and effectively prevented anyone from challenging him

The 'Three Antis' and 'Five Antis' movements

The 'Three Antis' movement

In 1951, Mao called for a 'big clean-up throughout the Party' and the Three Antis movement was launched. This was a campaign directed against corruption, waste and **obstructionist bureaucracy** in government. It had some public support from those who believed the official claims that it was aimed at ending corruption within the Party. It removed opponents of the Communists. People found that their friends and family members disappeared, never to be seen again. The Party also encouraged ordinary Chinese citizens to become involved in political activities with rallies organised to denounce 'counter-revolutionaries'. The victims were subjected to public **'struggle meetings'** where they were forced to admit their guilt in front of large crowds demanding retribution.

The 'Five Antis' movement

The CCP also used mass campaigns to remove possible opponents and seize control over economic assets. The 1952 Five Antis were against bribery, tax evasion, theft of state property, cheating on government contracts and stealing state economic information. The **bourgeoisie** and private business owners were targeted. So-called 'Tiger beaters', selected employees of a firm, were organised by the Party cadres into a team of activists and ordered to gather incriminating evidence against their former managers and bosses. The beaters intimidated the 'capitalist tigers', torturing them until they were dragged before a 'struggle meeting' and forced to confess their crimes. Many committed suicide to avoid being denounced.

Both campaigns were very successful. Businessmen found guilty during the Three and Five Antis campaigns were forced to pay heavy fines and, in order to pay them, had to sell stock to the state, creating joint public-private enterprises. The Party sent cadres into the companies to take on leading management roles, enhancing their control.

The use of terror against opponents of Communist rule

The CCP used the PLA to attack the bandit gangs that made travel across China so dangerous. Organised crime gangs like the **Triads** had plagued Chinese people for generations and the use of the army to crush them was very popular. Thousands of bandits and criminals were killed. The PLA intimidated their enemies and humiliated their families: when a criminal was executed a bill was sent to their parents to cover the cost of the bullets used in their execution.

The reunification campaigns in Tibet, Xinjiang and Guangdong

When they came to power in 1949, the Communists knew that they needed to establish control over all Chinese territory to make it safe from foreign interference or rival ideologies. Tibet followed a different belief system, Buddhism, and its people were loyal to an alternative leader, the **Dalai Lama**. The PLA attacked, Buddhist traditions were banned and the Dalai Lama was forced to flee. Similarly, Xinjiang province in the west had a large Muslim population with ethnic ties to some national groups in the Soviet Union. Mao feared that this would lead to Soviet interference within China's borders. Again, the PLA attacked and cleared all resistance by March 1950. In the south, Guangdong, which was an economically important port close to Hong Kong, was purged of Nationalist forces, who were forced to flee to Taiwan. An estimated 28,000 people were executed in Guangdong.

The development of the Laogai system

The Communists created a vast network of labour camps in order to imprison their enemies. They were called Laogai, meaning 'reform through labour'. By the start of 1955, there were more than 1.3 million people undergoing forced labour. Some prisoners were common criminals. However, most were political opponents of the regime or those whose class background and education made them suspect, like doctors or engineers. The inmates were forced to do hard labour. Conditions were terrible and death by disease was common. They were forced to attend meetings where they were brainwashed with Communist propaganda. Many committed suicide as the only way to escape.

RAG – Rate the timeline

Below is a sample exam-style question and a timeline. Read the question, study the timeline and, using three coloured pens, put a red, amber or green star next to the events to show:
- Red: events and policies that have no relevance to the question.
- Amber: events and policies that have some significance to the question.
- Green: events and policies that are directly relevant to the question.

How accurate is it to say that Communist control of China was entirely dependent on violent suppression of its opponents, 1949–53?

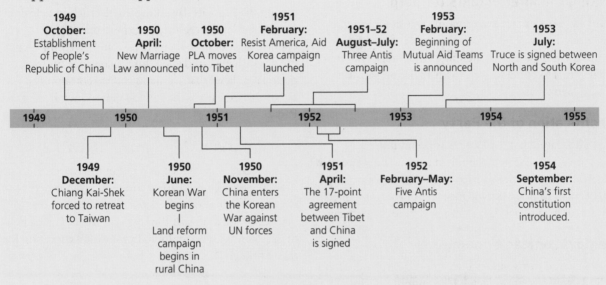

1949 October: Establishment of People's Republic of China

1950 April: New Marriage Law announced

1950 October: PLA moves into Tibet

1951 February: Resist America, Aid Korea campaign launched

1951–52 August–July: Three Antis campaign

1953 February: Beginning of Mutual Aid Teams is announced

1953 July: Truce is signed between North and South Korea

1949 | 1950 | 1951 | 1952 | 1953 | 1954 | 1955

1949 December: Chiang Kai-Shek forced to retreat to Taiwan

1950 June: Korean War begins | Land reform campaign begins in rural China

1950 November: China enters the Korean War against UN forces

1951 April: The 17-point agreement between Tibet and China is signed

1952 February–May: Five Antis campaign

1954 September: China's first constitution introduced.

Develop the detail

Below is a sample exam-style question and paragraph written in answer to this question. The paragraph contains a limited amount of detail. Annotate the paragraph to add additional detail to the answer.

How far do you agree that terror and violence were the most important factors in establishing Communist control of China in 1950–53?

Terror and violence were very significant factors in the establishment of Communist control in China in the period 1949–53. For example, the Three and Five Antis campaigns removed many opponents. This was popular with some people. It showed that the Communists would remove their enemies. The campaigns were boosted by the Korean War because the new government could use the war as an excuse. It was not just terror and violence that helped establish Communist control. Some Communist policies were popular with many Chinese people. Despite this, terror and violence were very significant because they spread fear and intimidated opponents into submission.

The Hundred Flowers campaign, 1957

Why did Mao launch the Hundred Flowers campaign?

During the Hundred Flowers campaign Mao appeared to encourage criticism of the Party by intellectuals, asking them to engage in a discussion and debate about future policies. Why did he do this?

Asking the intellectuals for help

Mao was worried that the economy was not improving fast enough. It may have been that the Hundred Flowers campaign was a genuine attempt to encourage educated intellectuals to come forward with advice and answers to this problem.

Rectification of the Party

Mao also feared that the Party was becoming less revolutionary: he feared that it had become **bureaucratic** and need to be 'rectified'. Mao wanted to encourage intellectuals to point out the mistakes of Party members and force them to act in the interests of the people again.

Removal of Mao's enemies

Mao believed that some members of the Party were not radical enough in introducing Communist policies, especially economic reforms which Mao wanted to happen very quickly. He hoped that the intellectuals would criticise these more conservative Communists, giving him the opportunity to remove them.

International concerns

In February 1956, the leader of the Soviet Union, **Nikita Khrushchev**, made a famous speech that denounced Stalin's **cult of personality**. This so-called '**Secret Speech**' criticised Stalin's use of the secret police and terror to intimidate and repress opponents. This might have made Mao nervous. He sought a way to prove that he was not a dictator by encouraging debate.

Over-confidence

Rather than feeling worried, it has been suggested that the Hundred Flowers Campaign started because Mao was actually feeling optimistic. The early years of the People's Republic of China (PRC) had been a success: the GMD had been forced to flee, the Korean War had been a success and the First Five-Year Plan (see page 32) had boosted industrialisation. Land reform had been popular among the peasants. By asking intellectuals to deliver a judgement on the regime, he expected a ringing endorsement of his policies that would give him even greater influence and allow him to advance his own personal policies that would introduce communism rapidly, against the wishes of less radical members of the Party.

Criticisms of Mao and the CCP

Emboldened, the intellectuals began to criticise the Party. They denounced the Party's failure to provide democratic rights or freedom of expression. They attacked the privileged situation that the Communist leaders had given themselves, with better food, housing and education for their children.

Mao's response

In June, Mao's speech on 'Handling Contradictions' was finally published in the *People's Daily* but there was no mention of compromise or moderation in this version. Instead it declared that 'poisonous weeds' had grown up among the 'fragrant flowers'. These '**right-wingers**' had abused their freedoms and he demanded a campaign of class struggle against them.

Aftermath of the Hundred Flowers campaign

Mao launched the 'Anti-Rightist' campaign. It is estimated that between 400,000 and 700,000 intellectuals were purged and sent to the countryside or the Laogai for 'labour reform'. Others committed suicide.

Support or challenge?

Below is a sample exam-style question that asks how far you agree with a specific statement. Below this is a series of general statements that are relevant to the question. Using your own knowledge and the information on the opposite page, decide whether these statements support or challenge the statement in the question and tick the appropriate box.

How accurate is it to say that Mao launched the Hundred Flowers campaign as a devious plan to trap his opponents?

Statement	Support	Challenge
Mao genuinely wanted to win the support of the intellectuals.		
As soon as the criticism came, Mao quickly launched the Anti-Rightist campaign.		
Mao knew that without the support of experts, economic production could not be increased.		
Mao was very worried by the 1956 Hungarian uprising.		
Mao viewed all intellectuals and experts as 'class enemies'.		
Mao was worried that the Party was becoming bureaucratic.		
Mao was shocked and depressed by the criticism that he received.		
Khrushchev's Secret Speech made Mao worried about looking too dictatorial.		
Mao honestly believed that the people were happy with the government.		

Simple essay style

Below is a sample exam question. Use your own knowledge and the information on the opposite page to produce a plan for this question. Choose four general points and provide three pieces of specific information to support each general point. Once you have planned your essay, write the introduction and conclusion for the essay. The introduction should list the points to be discussed in the essay. The conclusion should summarise the key points and justify which point was the most important.

How far do you agree that Mao launched the Hundred Flowers campaign in 1957 as a genuine attempt to encourage political debate?

China and the Korean War

On 25 June 1950, a 135,000-strong army of Communist North Korean troops invaded capitalist South Korea. When a coalition of UN forces, led by the superpower the United States, repelled the invasion and advanced close to the North Korean border with China, Mao Zedong took military action. The PRC, just a year old, was suddenly at war with 15 nations. Against great odds, the Chinese army, the PLA, fought the UN nations to a standstill. Hostilities ended with a ceasefire in 1953.

The war's role in enhancing CCP control, suppressing opposition and promoting national unity

There were a number of positives for the Communist regime from intervening in the Korean War:

- It helped enhance the power of the CCP. The PRC was just a year old when war broke out and the CCP desperately needed the support of Communist leaders in other countries to survive. By fighting a war against the capitalist Americans, Mao was able to prove to Stalin that he was a trustworthy ally.
- The war provided an excuse for the regime to lock up its enemies. The regime could denounce non-Communists as spies, capitalist sympathisers or traitors.
- The war gave the regime an excuse to enforce conscription, raise taxes and force farmers to give up their crops to aid the war effort.
- The Communists launched the 'Resist America, Aid Korea' campaign. This mobilised public support for the Chinese army by encouraging workers to donate wages for the war effort. This created a sense of shared national pride and unity.
- Mao clearly saw an opportunity to build popular support for his regime. If the Communist army, the PLA, could fight successfully against them, Mao would be viewed as a brave and heroic leader.

The human and financial costs of intervention in Korea

In 1950, China was still recovering from the catastrophic impacts of invasion by the Japanese, the Second World War and the Civil War. The new regime desperately needed a period of stability. Instead the war had a terrible impact on the Chinese economy and the lives of the Chinese people.

The human cost of the war

Of the 3 million Chinese soldiers sent to Korea, 400,000 died. In China, the forced requisition of grain to supply the armed forces led to famine in some parts of the country. Launched in March 1950, the campaign to suppress counter-revolutionaries was aimed at preventing Nationalist sympathisers and their spies from undermining the regime. Most vulnerable were those who had worked for the previous Nationalist regime and academics who had worked with foreign universities. Businessmen were forced to leave the country and had their property confiscated, while many Christian missionaries were arrested.

The financial cost of the war

As a result of the money spent on the war, much-needed reforms in education, health care, transport and infrastructure did not happen. The government did negotiate military support from the Soviet Union, but this aid was not free and had to be paid back. The war cost the PRC $10 billion.

China's enhanced international prestige

China had previously been viewed as 'the sick man of Asia', a backward nation bullied and humiliated by foreign powers. In contrast, military success in the war meant China was now feared and respected in the West.

Spectrum of importance

Below is a sample exam-style question and a list of general points that could be used to answer the question. Use your own knowledge and the information in this section so far to reach a judgement about the importance of these general points to the question posed. Write numbers on the spectrum below to indicate their relative importance. Then write a brief justification of your placement, explaining why some of these factors are more important than others. The resulting diagram could form the basis of an essay plan.

How far do you agree that the Korean War helped Mao establish Communist control over China?

1 The Resist America, Aid Korea campaign

2 The impact of the war on the Chinese economy

3 The effect on the personal prestige of Mao

4 The impact on national pride

5 International reactions with other countries

6 The military results of the war

Least important   Most important

The flaw in the argument

Below is a sample exam question and a paragraph written in answer to this question. The paragraph contains an argument which attempts to answer the question. However, there is an error in the argument. Use your knowledge of this topic to identify the flaw in the argument.

How accurate is it to say that Chinese involvement in the Korean War was largely beneficial to the people of China?

The Chinese people benefited greatly from the Korean War. First, Mao gained great prestige from fighting the combined forces of the United Nations to a standstill. Secondly, the people were spurred on by a great feeling of patriotism and national pride. For years, China had been viewed as the 'sick man of Asia' and was humiliated by the European nations. Chinese workers contributed their wages to help the war effort, which brought all the Chinese people together and created a sense of national unity against a common enemy. Now China had, in Mao's words, 'stood up'. Third, the war provided the opportunity to identify 'enemy spies and agents', such as anyone educated in the West or members of religions like Christianity. They were removed during the 'Resist America, Aid Korea' campaign.

Exam focus – AS question

Look at the exam questions below, then read the answers and the comments around them.

How much weight do you give to the evidence of Source 1 for an enquiry into the success of the Communist government's policies in the years 1950–53? Explain your answer using the source, the information given about it and your own knowledge of the historical context.

SOURCE 1

'Democratic Reform in Factories and Mines' published in Workers' Daily, *12 September 1951. This article, published in a pro-Communist workers' newspaper, reports on the introduction of Communist reforms into factories.*

The first step is democratic struggle ... we should carry out struggles of reasoning at mass meetings. These struggles will be directed against 'number ones', heads of reactionary religious societies, leaders of secret brotherhoods and backbones of reactionary parties and youth corps, who 'earned their positions not by their merits, but by their backgrounds', who never or seldom took part in production and who rode on the heads of the workers and exercised feudal oppression and exploitation. There may be persons whose offenses were of a serious nature, who have incurred public hatred. These people may be sent to people's courts for trial. At this stage the main hesitation of the laboring classes is fear of insufficient backing from the leadership. The most important thing to observe is to inform the masses of the policy and procedure to be pursued and then encourage discussion and full expression from the lower ranks upwards. Do not pull strings or dominate the workers. In factories, railways and mines where the masses have been fully mobilized, a new attitude toward labour has been formed among workers, labour discipline has been strengthened and efficiency has increased. Yet production targets which had been fulfilled in the past were overfulfilled on time.

Source 1 can be attributed a moderate degree of weight as evidence of the policies introduced by the Communist government in the years 1950–53. However, the utility of the source is reduced because it focuses only on one area of policy, namely the use of terror, and because its purpose is to show the new Communist government only in a good light by exaggerating the policies' success.

In terms of context, the source is useful in showing how the Communists were attempting to purge their enemies in the first years after they came to power. They wanted to increase factory production and modernise what was a mainly backward, agricultural economy. The Communists believed that this was being prevented by 'reactionary enemies'. These included religious groups such as Christians, who the Communists believed were loyal to a 'bourgeois' ideology or, in the case of the Catholics, a rival leader in the Pope. The source also refers to the need to remove 'secret brotherhoods' – these were the secret societies and criminal gangs like the Triads, who had gained great influence and power when the government had been weak. The source is also useful in that it reveals the Communist motivation of the regime: one of the offences of their enemies was that they exploited the workers, while they themselves 'seldom or never took part in production.' These enemies were bourgeois and corrupt – they had not 'earned their positions by merit' but 'by their background'. Before 1949, China had been a very unequal society. Corrupt factory owners had become rich through exploiting their positions. The Communists had won support with their promise to make society more equal and this source suggests how this desire motivated the repressive treatment of their enemies.

Clear, focused judgement regarding the weight of the source.

Balanced argument, clearly stating how the utility of the source is altered by its limitations based on its origin and purpose.

Source and own knowledge integrated – source quotation is explained using detailed example.

A clear focus on utility of source with judgement based on reference to its 'motivation'.

The source holds great value in showing how the Communists used terror and violence to establish their control. They used 'mass mobilisation' to attack their enemies. This concept was a key aspect of 'Mao Zedong Thought' and is clear evidence of how Mao's personal ideology inspired policy. The Communist government sent Party cadres into factories to encourage workers to organise the 'struggles ... at mass meetings'. At the meetings, workers denounced their bosses for 'feudal oppression' and many were beaten or even killed. The source argues that the policies were most effective when the workers took ownership of the violence and organised their own 'struggle meetings'. The Party cadres should not 'dominate' but should simply encourage 'full expression'. This policy was effective in building support for the regime because it gave the workers a sense of empowerment after being oppressed. It built support because it implicated the people in the activities of the regime: they had blood on their hands, and this made them more desperate to prevent a return to power of the 'feudal enemies' because if this happened, those guilty workers would be punished. These struggle meetings gave the impression that workers were important and had power and influence, but they were also excellent propaganda for spreading fear and intimidating the new regime's opponents. Therefore, the source has value in that it makes clear that the regime was engaged in a class war against its enemies. It does provide a balanced argument when it admits that the workers have been afraid to denounce their enemies because they fear that they might not be supported by the Communist leadership.

However, in terms of provenance, the source holds limited weight. It was published in the *Workers' Daily*, a pro-Communist newspaper. It exaggerates the danger posed by the ideological enemies like the religious groups or criminal gangs in order to justify the use of struggle meetings and terror. It also greatly exaggerates the impact of the campaign in improving economic production. The source is a piece of propaganda that focuses only upon the positives of and popular support for the Communist policies. It underplays the brutal nature of the struggle meetings: it refers to punishments such as 'demotion' or 'reduction in salary'. In fact, many struggle meetings got out of control and victims were taken away to the new prison camp network, the Laogai. Others were simply murdered, while some victims, threatened with being dragged before a struggle meeting, committed suicide. The purpose of the source is to convince readers that the regime's policies were genuinely popular and effective. It does not provide a complete picture of the repressive realities of the new regime's policies. It refers to a 'new attitude' and that 'labour discipline' has been improved, but fails to mention that this improvement had been enforced through repressive measures. For example, it fails to mention other aspects of control in the factories such as the imposition of the Danwei, the work units that all workers were forced to join and which controlled access to permits to travel or get married and to food supplies and housing. It is correct that 'efficiency has increased' but this was in part due to force and control.

In conclusion, the source does have value in that it reveals the class war motivations of Communist policies and the way the won support for these policies through mass mobilisation. However, to gain a more balanced understanding of Communist policies, the historian should use the source in conjunction with other sources with less of a pro-Communist political purpose to exaggerate the support and effectiveness of the policies.

A further way in which the source is of value is introduced.

Judgement on the value of the source based on how 'balanced' it is.

Judgement on limitations of the source's weight, rooted in analysis of its provenance.

Limitations of source addressed with reference to both what it exaggerates and what it underplays.

A nuanced conclusion that clarifies the judgement of weight, but also suggests what a historian would have to do in order to make use of the source for this particular question.

This answer is awarded a mark in Level 5 because it shows an understanding of how the provenance of the source impacts upon its utility and its 'weight' as historical evidence. It also uses information from the source very effectively, using well-selected quotations to build an argument. The conclusion ends with a judgement that suggests what a historian might need to do to enhance their understanding of the Communist government's polices.

Consolidation

These answers demand a combination of argument, own knowledge and reference to sources. Colour code each of these three components.

Exam focus – AS question

REVISED

Study Source 2 before you answer the following exam-style question.

How valuable is Source 2 for an enquiry into how the CCP established its political control of China, 1950–53? Explain your answer using the source, the information given about it and your own knowledge of the historical context.

SOURCE 2

From Zhisui Li, The Private Life of Chairman Mao, (Arrow books, 1996). This is a memoir by Zhisui Li, Mao's private doctor for over twenty years. The book is banned in China.

When the Korean War broke out in the summer of 1950, I volunteered. I had not participated in the war of resistance against Japan or in the civil war against the nationalists, but I wanted to serve my country, even though I was certain that China would be defeated. The United States was so much more advanced than China, and American equipment was better. I followed the war closely, surprised and thrilled that China was not only holding its own but was actually defeating the United States in battle after battle. It was the first time in more than a century that China was engaged in war with a foreign power without losing face. I was appalled, too, over reports that the United States was using bacteriological warfare in Korea. Even as the Korean War dragged on inconclusively, I was proud to be Chinese. But my superiors refused to allow me to participate, arguing again that my services were more valuable in Zhongnanhai. I became depressed, frustrated at not being allowed to contribute to the revolution, disappointed at not being able to continue my career as a surgeon. I felt remote from the revolutionaries who were patients and unhappy that my application for membership in the Party was so long delayed … They were also suspicious because part of my internship after medical school had been spent working as a military doctor under the Guomindang.

The source clearly has some value for an enquiry into the ways that the Communist Party established its control over China. Indeed, it is an eyewitness account of someone living in China at the time. It is especially useful because the author worked at the political headquarters of the CCP and so was well placed to comment upon the establishment of Party control. However, the author is clearly a supporter of the CCP, and does not consider the use of violence and terror to establish control. This was a key aspect of the development of Mao's dictatorship and lack of reference to this clearly limits the value of the source.

The source is very useful as evidence of the importance of the Korean War for the establishment of CCP control. The CCP was able to use the war to build support for the new regime: after years of being humiliated by foreign nations, the Communist armies made

This is a focused introduction that sets out a range of ways in which the source can be used, including reference to its value and also its limitations.

many Chinese people feel proud because they fought the United States, one of the world's superpowers, to a standstill. The CCP turned the success of the PLA into a propaganda victory, using it as evidence of the ideological superiority of Communism and building a sense of patriotism and national unity that had not existed in China before. The 'Resist America, Aid Korea' campaign successfully mobilised the people in support of Communism. The PLA became role models to be aspired to and Mao was able to use the war to begin to build his cult of personality.

The source is also useful because it was written by Mao's personal doctor. It is clear that he was a supporter of the Communists. This is no reason to dismiss the source. On the contrary, a doctor would have been educated and potentially targeted by the regime as a class enemy. The source alludes to this when it refers to the Party's suspicions about his past medical training and experience as a military doctor. Despite this, the source provides excellent evidence about the popular support for the regime. One might expect an educated, middle class professional like Dr Li to oppose the regime, but instead he supports it. This is evidence that the regime enjoyed at least some cross-class support when it first came to power. However, Dr Li's example should not be viewed as representative of all of the middle classes: many did not support the regime and fled to Taiwan with the Guomindang.

Finally, the source fails to discuss the fact that the regime established its control through terror and violence. During the early days of the regime the Three and Five Antis campaigns attacked opponents, subjecting them to 'struggle meetings' where they were publicly denounced. Many were sent to the new labour camps, the Laogai, a vast prison network modelled upon Stalin's gulags The source mentions the popular support gained by the regime because of the Korean War, but it fails to mention that during the war it was used to legitimise the purging of opponents on the pretence that they were spies or traitors, the repression of those educated at Western universities and the expulsion of Western religious missionaries.

In conclusion, the source is partly useful. As an eyewitness account it is likely to be accurate about the support for the regime. The fact that it is written by someone who might, because of his background, be politically motivated to actually oppose the regime only adds to its weight. However, the source may not be representative and is clearly limited as it does not consider the importance of terror and violence in establishing Communist control in the first years of the regime.

> Here the essay uses knowledge of the historical context of the Korean War to evaluate the usefulness of Dr Li's argument.

> The value of Dr Li's argument is evaluated in terms of his class background.

> The overall value is weighed up and evaluated in terms of valid criteria and the conclusion distinguishes between the different ways in which the source can be used.

The answer makes clear judgements on the utility of the source based on analysis of its provenance. The answer makes the limitation of the source clear, with direct reference to its provenance. Supporting factual knowledge is well selected and utilised to support judgements.

Exam focus activity

This essay is successful because it maintains a strong focus on the question throughout. There is a lot of detail on various elements but other paragraphs are also related to political control where possible. Go through the essay and underline every mention of the words 'political control'. Next look at an essay you have written and underline your use of key words. Can you improve on your own efforts in the light of what you have seen here?

Exam focus – A-level question

Read the exam-style question and model answer below.

How far could the historian make use of Sources 3 and 4 together to investigate the consequences of the 'anti' movements of 1951–52? Explain your answer, using both sources, the information given about them and your own knowledge of the historical context.

SOURCE 3

From Escape from Red China, *by Robert Loh. Loh was a Chinese citizen who lived and studied in the United States before he returned to China in 1949, believing that he would be able to help rebuild China.*

When the Party Secretary received my seventh confession he remarked, 'At last, I believe your confession is relatively thorough. But the final verdict, of course, is with the masses. You will now write out an expression of your attitude concerning your crimes.' I had read and heard the expected 'expression of attitude' often enough so that I was able to write one myself without effort. A few hours after finishing it, I faced the climax of my 'struggle'. The tiger beaters propelled me roughly into the mills' dining hall. My entrance was the signal for a tremendous uproar. The screams of rage, the shouted slogans, the insults, were deafening. My knees trembled with both weakness and fear. One by one, representatives from each of the employee groups came to the stage to denounce me. The worst accusations were made by those whom I had known best. I could see the pain in the eyes of some as they stumbled over their memorised speeches. I read my confession in a weak voice. I thanked the great Communist Party which, under the wise and benevolent leadership of Chairman Mao, had instigated this great campaign.

SOURCE 4

From directives written for the Central Committee by Mao Zedong on 5 March 1952. The directives were issued during the Five Antis movement.

In some big and medium-sized cities, the Party committees launched the movement against the 'five evils' in a hurry. They were not acquainted with the situation with respect to the different categories of industrial and commercial units. 'Work Teams' sent by the trade unions and the government had been organized in a very slipshod way. As a result some confusion has arisen. It is hoped that the city Party committees concerned will pay attention to this situation and see to its correction without delay. The investigation of industrial and commercial units which break the law must be made under the strict control of the city Party committee and the city government. No other organization is allowed to send out people to investigate on its own, much less to haul capitalists into its office for interrogation. Whether in the movement against the 'three evils' or against the 'five evils', the use of torture to extort confessions is forbidden. Where suicides have occurred, measures for preventing their further occurrence should be worked out immediately.

Both sources are useful to a historian investigating the 'anti' movements of 1951–52 because they deal with the political consequences of the campaign and come from radically different perspectives. Source 3 was written by Robert Loh, a Chinese-born intellectual and not a Communist. It is a public document written to expose the cruelties of Communist rule, after the author managed to escape. Source 4, in contrast, was written during the campaign, a private document intended for senior CCP officials. The two sources allow the historian to see the consequences of the 'anti' movements from radically different angles. However, neither source deals with the consequences for the government or the economy. Therefore, there are limits to how much of the impact of the movements a historian could uncover.

Both sources are useful as they indicate that the campaigns were used to intimidate people. Source 3 describes the public denunciation of opponents at 'struggle meetings' and how Loh 'trembled with fear'. It refers to how the demands of confessions were unrelenting: he states that he was forced to write no less than seven confessions, implying this interrogation and humiliation lasted

Clear focus on the question.

Initial contrast between the nature, origin and purpose of the sources.

Initial judgement on limitations of the sources for the enquiry.

a long time. Loh's account is supported by Source 4 where Mao describes enemies being 'hauled' out for 'interrogation'. Indeed, the 'anti' campaigns were conducted in the context of anti-capitalist fervour, due to the 'Resist America, Aid Korea' campaign during which those accused of being enemies were subjected to a public meeting where 'insults and slogans', were used which caused Loh to become 'weak at the knees'. As someone who had lived abroad, in the USA, Loh would definitely have been a target of suspicion during these campaigns. Source 3 is also useful as it suggests that people were forced to denounce people they knew to be innocent. This was a key aspect of mass campaigns: they created an atmosphere of fear and mistrust that helped prevent opposition to the regime.

Judgement of utility of Source 3, based on the background of the author.

The reliability of Source 3 might be questioned as Loh's purpose was to expose the violence of Communist rule. Loh was of middle-class background and had been educated in the USA. However, there is no doubt that many of the middle classes at the time were subjected to this kind of struggle meeting. A Western-educated intellectual would definitely come under scrutiny. Therefore, Loh's purpose should not mean that we reject his interpretation. It is an eyewitness account that can be verified by evidence that thousands were subjected to struggle meetings and purged at the time. Source 4 is useful as it gives an official view of the consequences of the movements. Mao's tone is critical of Party members and trade unionists. The directives imply the campaigns were not carried out as they were intended, and zealots were out of control. It is not clear to what extent Mao's instructions in Source 4 were carried out. It is quite plausible that ambitious Party cadres would have ignored his instructions, especially if they could benefit. Indeed, uncontrolled violence beyond that envisaged by the Party leadership took place during the land reform campaigns and the Great Leap Forward.

Source 3 used to evaluate the utility of Source 4.

Source 4 refers to 'the use of torture to extort confessions' and capitalists being dragged off for 'interrogation' by people who had no authority. This is clearly supported by Source 3, which describes just such a meeting. These claims are plausible, as Mao oversaw the campaign. Mao's reference to 'suicides' as a consequence of the movements is also plausible. Furthermore, Source 4 refers to the need to prevent further suicides: from this we can infer that the intimidation had become so bad that so many people had committed suicide that Mao had to personally intervene. It is estimated around 200,000 people committed suicide due to the campaigns. Mao's claim that unexpected 'confusion has arisen', leading Party and union members to act irresponsibly, is less plausible. Mao argues that the 'anti' movements were based on 'different categories'. However, the 'anti' movements were 'campaigns', which demanded that victims appear before the 'masses' to 'beg for forgiveness' (Source 3), rather than clear bureaucratic administration. Party cadres were sent into factories – the 'tiger beaters' (Source 3) – to encourage workers to denounce their former bosses. This process was established and used with great effect during the land reform programmes instituted before and after 1949. Therefore, it is not plausible for Mao to argue that confusion about official categories was an unexpected consequence because of the nature of mass campaigns. However, Mao's instructions may indicate that the consequences of the campaigns, particularly the violence and suicides, were greater than anticipated.

Understanding of the context of the period is used in order to discuss the limitations of the source.

Interrogation of the source. Reasoned inferences help distinguish between the different types of material in the source.

Finally, both sources are of quite limited use because neither deal with the consequences that Mao had initially envisaged. The 'Three Antis' campaign was designed to remove GMD sympathisers from government, while the 'Five Antis' campaign was designed to increased CCP control of the economy ahead of the First Five-Year Plan. Neither source deals explicitly with the extent to which these aims were met.

Limitations of sources clearly addressed.

Overall, both sources are useful as they provide plausible evidence that the campaigns had violent consequences. However, Mao's claim that the campaigns had become confused because they had slipped out of the 'strict control' of the Party is implausible because they were always intended to be mass campaigns. Finally, the sources are limited as neither deals explicitly with the intended consequences of the 'anti' movements.

Conclusion presents a focused summary of the essay, and distinguishes between the degrees of certainty with which aspects of the sources can be used to make claims.

This is a Level 5 answer. It interrogates the evidence of both sources with confidence and deploys contextual knowledge to highlight their value and limitations.

2 Agricultural and industrial changes, 1949–65

Early changes in agriculture, 1949–57

What were Mao's main aims for agriculture?

- Mao needed to increase food supplies to the cities to feed the workers in his new factories.
- However, he was very wary of exploiting the peasants too much: he knew how unpopular the Communists in the Soviet Union had become when they had requisitioned too much grain from the peasants and decided to **collectivise** their land.
- In a country that was still largely made up of poor peasants, he knew that he needed an agricultural policy that would both increase supplies and enhance the popularity of Communism in the countryside.
- Only when China was economically strong could Mao make good on his claim that the 'Chinese people had stood up'.

Attacks on landlordism

The Communists viewed China's landowners as feudal class enemies. They would need to be destroyed to allow the Communists to continue to redistribute land to the peasants, a policy that was their greatest source of support and something that they had already been doing before 1949. Work Teams of Party cadres were sent to villages to encourage peasants to drag their local landlords before 'struggle meetings' where they would be denounced for exploiting their tenants and forced to give up their land. The Communists whipped up anger against them, in some cases releasing years of pent-up petty jealously and long-festering resentments. Some were sentenced to death.

The redistribution of land

Introduced in 1950, the Agrarian Reform Law stated that a 'system of peasant land ownership shall be introduced'. This country-wide land reform removed legal protection from landlords, leaving them powerless to keep hold of their land. Sometimes the violence escalated beyond that encouraged by the Work Teams, with peasants seeing the opportunity to settle old scores and family feuds, or simply a chance to seize more land from a well-off neighbour and improve their standard of living. By the summer of 1952, 43 per cent of the land had been redistributed to 60 per cent of the population. Rural production boomed: between 1950 and 1952 total agricultural production increased at a rate of 15 per cent per annum. The cost had been an estimated 1 to 2 million landlords executed.

Spot the inference   a

High-level answers avoid excessive summarising or paraphrasing of the sources. They instead make inferences from the sources, as well as analysing their value in terms of their context. Below is a source and a series of statements. Read the source and decide which of the statements:

- make inferences from the source (I)
- paraphrase the source (P)
- summarise the source (S)
- cannot be justified from the source (X).

Statement	I	P	S	X
Land reform benefited the peasants economically.				
Poorer peasants took advantage of the land reform programme to exploit landlords.				
The land reform programme turned the peasants into ideologically committed Communists.				
The peasants kept on demanding money and food from the landlords until finally they gave them everything. This greatly improved the life of the peasants.				

SOURCE 1

From William Hinton, Fanshen: A Documentary of Revolution in a Chinese Village *(Random House, 1968), pages 137–38. The source describes a 'struggle meeting' that took place in 1949. The victim was a local landlord, Ching-ho.*

Old women who had never spoken in public before stood up to accuse him. Even Li Mao's wife … shook her fist before his nose and cried out, 'Once I went to glean [gather] wheat on your land. But you cursed me and drove me away.' Altogether over 180 opinions were raised. Ching-ho had no answer to them. He stood there with his head bowed. When the committee of our Association met to figure up what he owed, it came to 400 bags of milled grain. We went in to register his grain and altogether found but 200 bags of unmilled millet. [We] asked him what he intended to do since the grain was not nearly enough. He said, 'I have land and a house.' 'But all this is not enough', shouted the people. So then we began to beat him. Finally he said, 'I have 40 silver dollars.' We went in and dug it up. We beat him again. He told us where to find another hundred after that. Several militiamen began to heat an iron bar in one of the fires. Altogether we got $500 from Ching-ho. All said: 'In the past we never lived through a happy New Year because he always asked for his rent and interest then and cleaned our houses bare. This time we'll eat what we like' and everyone ate his fill and didn't even notice the cold.

Moves towards agricultural co-operation

The redistribution of land to the peasants was only the first step towards the creation of a Communist society in towns and the countryside. The CCP had no intention of replacing one landlord class with another, and regarded land reform as only the first stage of a comprehensive package of agricultural reforms.

In 1951, the Party introduced Mutual Aid Teams (MATs). These teams organised peasants into teams of 10 or fewer households. They shared resources like tools, fertilisers and animals, and pooled their labour for the benefit of the whole community. This helped poorer peasants. MATs were effective and popular. The buying and selling of land and hiring of labourers was still allowed.

Agricultural Producers' Co-operatives

The next stage was the creation of Agricultural Producers' Co-operatives (APCs). They were made up of 30 to 50 households. Although land remained in private ownership, local parties reorganised landholdings into larger units which could be farmed more efficiently and profitably. The state took a share of the harvest and the peasants then received money or grain back in payment. Many richer peasants did not want to join and slaughtered their animals rather than give them to the APC. The results were disappointing. In 1953 and 1954, grain production rose by less than 2 per cent. Mao knew that there would be resistance: 'The peasants want freedom, but we want socialism', he admitted.

The change from voluntary to enforced collectivisation

The failure of APCs gave rise to disagreements within the Party over the pace of agricultural change. Conservative opponents of rapid change, like Lui Shaoqi and Premier Zhou Enlai, claimed that China was not yet ready for large-scale farming because of the lack of mechanised equipment such as tractors and combine harvesters. They also knew what had happened in the USSR when Stalin had tried to introduce rapid collectivisation, so they proposed a slow, step-by-step approach. Mao disagreed. In July 1955, he demanded an increase in the pace of reform towards full collectivisation and an end to all private property. In December 1955, 63.3 per cent of peasant households were part of an APC, with 4 per cent of those being Higher-Level APCs comprising two to three hundred households, sometimes encompassing whole villages. By January 1956, 80.3 per cent of peasant households were in APCs, and by now 30.7 per cent of those were Higher-Level APCs. Now pragmatism was completely abandoned. Private ownership was abolished. Members would only be compensated for their labour: their land and equipment were simply taken over by the state. In these new APCs tools, all equipment and land were to be shared. Membership was now compulsory. Except for some very small private plots, privately owned land ceased to exist and no compensation was provided. By the end of 1956, almost 88 per cent of peasants were in Higher-Level APCs.

RAG – Rate the timeline

Below is a sample exam-style question and a timeline. Read the question, study the timeline and, using three coloured pens, put a red, amber or green star next to the events to show:

● Red: events and policies that have no relevance to the question.

● Amber: events and policies that have some significance to the question.

● Green: events and policies that are directly relevant to the question.

How far did Chinese agriculture improve in the years 1949–57?

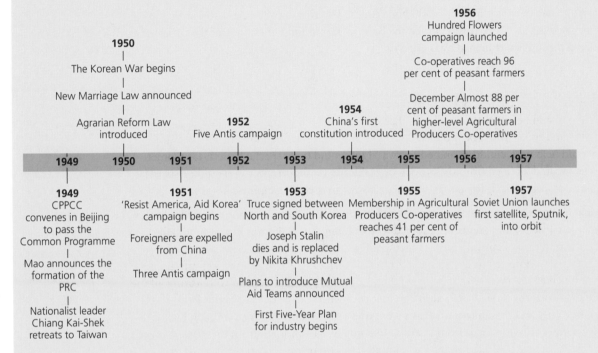

Now repeat the activity with the following questions.

How far do you agree that agrarian reform was a disaster for the Chinese people?

'Mao's popularity was based on his agricultural policy.' How far do you agree with this judgement?

Support your judgement

Below is a sample exam question and two basic judgements. Read the exam question and the two judgements. Support the judgement that you agree with more strongly by adding a reason that justifies the judgement.

'The CCP's agricultural policies in the years 1949–57 failed to improve the state of Chinese agriculture.' How far do you agree with this statement?

Collectivisation meant that the Chinese peasantry had no incentive to work hard to increase agricultural output.

Under collectivisation the state now owned all agricultural land, and could plan ways to increase the amount of food which was grown.

The communes

The organisation of the communes

By 1956, Mao was pleased with the creation of the co-operatives. He believed that the Party should introduce the next stage of collectivisation, the movement into massive communes. He believed that the progress made with MATs and APCs was a signal that his desire to increase the pace of collectivisation, in contrast to the cautionary pace advocated by his colleagues, was correct. He organised the peasants into communes. They would increase both agricultural and industrial production, a policy he called 'Walking on Two Legs'. The communes were vast: they had an average size of approximately 5,500 households. The first commune was organised in Henan province in July 1958. It was named the Sputnik Commune in honour of the first ever satellite, which had been launched by the USSR.

Communal living

Mao believed that the standard of living of the peasants would improve on the communes because they would be self-sufficient. Items that were in constant short supply, such as toothbrushes and rope, would be produced. Mess halls would provide food and crèches and schools would help with childcare and education. This would be of special benefit for women because they would be freed from the burden of childcare. Grandparents too would be spared from looking after grandchildren, enjoying their old age in special 'happiness homes'.

Communal living was a disaster, however. Abandoning their children to poorly organised crèches with under-qualified staff, parents were forced to work long hours. Eating in vast food halls destroyed the tradition of families eating together. The food was poor and diets worsened. Women were now expected to undertake harsh physical labour. When production still did not increase as much as Mao wanted, he believed that the reason was that vermin were eating all the grain. He organised the 'Four Pests' campaign that compelled the peasants to exterminate sparrows, rats, flies and mosquitoes. Peasants were told to bang pots and pans or bang drums to scare the sparrows and stop them from landing. Eventually, the birds fell from the sky, exhausted. Unfortunately, the sparrows ate insects and without them there was a plague of locusts that ate the harvest.

The abolition of private farming

By the end of 1958, the Party claimed that 99 per cent of the peasant population had been moved into communes. This represented almost half a billion people. Private ownership of land was outlawed. Livestock could not be owned: animals had to be shared with the commune. The selling of private produce was denounced by the Party as evidence of 'rural capitalism'. All markets where farmers could make extra money through selling produce were banned. Every commune organised a militia that controlled the people and prevented them from selling any food or goods. The private farming system that had dominated Chinese rural life for generations was completely destroyed.

Lysenkoism

Trofim Lysenko was a Soviet agrobiologist whose ideas had been supported by Stalin in the 1930s. In the mid-1950s, Mao adopted many of Lysenko's ideas and made them official government policy. Some of the methods advocated were catastrophic for Chinese agriculture. For example, Lysenko claimed, incorrectly, that crop yields would be increased if seeds were exposed to moisture and low temperatures before they were planted deep in the ground and close together. Lysenkoism proved to be utterly fraudulent, causing crop yields to fall dramatically and helping to unleash the disastrous famine of 1958–62.

Establish criteria

Below is a sample exam question which requires you to make a judgement. The key term in the question has been underlined. Defining the meaning of the key term can help you establish criteria that you can use to make a judgement.

Read the question, define the key term and then set out two or three criteria based on the key term which you can use to reach and justify a judgement.

> 'The communes brought <u>widespread</u> improvements to the lives of the Chinese people.' How far do you agree with this statement?

Definition:

_____

_____

Criteria to judge the extent to which communes brought widespread improvements to the lives of the Chinese people:

_____

_____

Develop the detail

Below is a sample exam question and a paragraph written in answer to this question. The paragraph contains a limited amount of detail. Annotate the paragraph to add additional detail to the answer.

> 'Mao's agricultural policies in the years 1949–57 were disastrous for the Chinese peasantry.' How far do you agree with this statement?

Mao was interested in imposing Communist rule in the countryside rather than improving the output of food for the Chinese people. People's lives were strongly controlled in the communes and their everyday life was very difficult. Lysenko's theories had a terrible impact, and peasants were forced to hunt down vermin which were destroying crops. There was hardly any increase in agricultural output between 1949 and 1957.

The Great Famine, 1958–62

With the peasants having little incentive to work hard, exhausted by long hours of work or chasing vermin in the 'Four Pests' campaign, agricultural production dropped drastically. However, the Party cadres in the communes did not want to be seen as failures or to criticise the communes – after all, they had seen what had happened during the Hundred Flowers campaign (see page 14) – so they greatly inflated their reports of what the communes had produced. In turn, their bosses in the Party, believing that there was plenty of food, set even higher production quotas. So bad was the misunderstanding that land was left fallow because the Party believed that there would be too much food to store, while 'excess' food was sent abroad to fellow Communist countries as free gifts. A terrible famine was the result.

Life during the Great Famine

The **Great Famine** was the worst recorded famine of the twentieth century. Eight million people starved to death in Anhui province, 7.8 million in Henan and 9 million in Sichuan. One million people died in Tibet. Starving peasants launched desperate attacks on food stores. Anyone discovered trying to steal food was sentenced to death. Birth rates plummeted as women's fertility dropped. Many, particularly children and the elderly, died of diseases they could not resist because of malnourishment. People ate frogs, worms or the bark from trees. There were outbreaks of cannibalism and men sold their wives into prostitution for food. The famine was made worse by terrible weather including flooding in South China and drought in Shandong. Although exact figures are unknown, it is estimated that approximately 30–50 million people died.

How far was Mao responsible for the Great Famine?

How far Mao was to blame for the Great Famine remains a source of debate between historians. Chang and Halliday (2005) blame Mao for bringing 'utter misery' by ordering **grain requisitioning** and continuing to export food even after the famine had begun. Other historians, like Jin Xiadoing, blame the famine on over-ambitious Party cadres who claimed to have collected more grain than they had in order to gain favour with their bosses. This might have been poor judgement, admits Jin, but 'bad judgement is not the same as starving people to death'. Mao himself blamed the weather, which was particularly bad. Although Mao did not control the lies of the Party cadres, it was ultimately he who created an atmosphere within which they were terrified for their own lives if they failed to meet their targets or even simply questioned Mao's policies.

The restoration of private farming by Liu Shaoqi and Deng Xiaoping

The famine was an embarrassment to Mao, and Liu Shaoqi and Deng Xiaoping took greater control over the running of the country. Pragmatists, they quickly moved to restore farming. They replaced 'Walking on Two Legs' with the motto 'Agriculture as the foundation of the economy'. Communes were reduced in size and peasants were allowed to farm small private plots. If they found unused land, they were allowed to farm on it. They could decide what to grow and how much fertiliser to use. They could trade their food at markets. The Party sent emergency supplies of insecticides, fertilisers and tools to the farms. By 1965, agricultural production had recovered from the disastrous Great Leap Forward (see page 34), returning to the same level as 1957.

Complete the paragraph

Below are a sample exam question and a paragraph written in answer to this question. The paragraph contains a point and specific examples, but lacks a concluding analytical link back to the question. Complete the paragraph by adding this link in the space provided.

'Mao's policies were entirely responsible for the Great Famine.' How far do you agree with this judgement?

> The Great Famine was caused by a number of factors. Moving the peasants into communes removed their incentive to work hard because they had to share everything they grew. They wasted a huge amount of time travelling across the commune to the food hall instead of going home to eat. The weather was particularly bad and there were droughts in some areas of China and floods in others. It is not exactly clear how many people died, but it was likely more than 30 million. It was only when Mao was sidelined and Liu and Deng began to control policy that the famine came to an end. They introduced a more pragmatic than ideological approach to agricultural policy and this helped China recover from the famine.

Explain the difference

The following sources give different accounts of conditions in the Chinese countryside in the years 1958–62. List the ways in which the sources differ. Explain the differences between the sources using the provenance of the sources and the historical context. The provenance appears at the top of each source. Make sure you stay focused on the differences that are relevant to the question.

How far could the historian make use of Sources 1 and 2 together to investigate conditions in the Chinese countryside in the years 1958–62? Explain your answer, using both sources, the information given about them and your own knowledge of the historical context.

SOURCE 1

Adapted from an article in the Peking Review, *8 September 1959. The Peking Review was an official CCP publication.*

In September 1958, the people's communes had only just begun in a few areas in China. Now they have been established in all rural areas. The Communist Party stressed that participation by the peasants must be voluntary and said 'compulsion is to be avoided'. The warm welcome given to the people's commune movement by the peasants, and the correct guidance given to it by the Party, led to its rapid upsurge throughout the country. In less than two months, the mass of the peasants set up more than 26,000 people's communes. The community dining rooms, the nurseries and the 'homes of respect for the aged' have played an important role in freeing women for productive work and improving the living standards of the peasants. During the summer this year, although the weather was bad, we got an even bigger harvest than that of 1958, the year of the Great Leap Forward.

SOURCE 2

'The Two-Line Struggle in Lien–Chiang County'. This source comes from an inner-Party report on life in the countryside in Fukien in 1962. Never meant for public attention, it was captured by the GMD and smuggled to Taiwan, where it was released.

First, there has been a recovery and an expansion in all phases of production, in agriculture, fishing and forestry ... The area occupied by the collectives has decreased by more than 20,000 mou since last year, principally because of an increase in private plots and vegetable farming. Second, there has been an increase in the standard of living of the masses. The level of their food rations was better this year than last. The masses say 'Life is better from year to year'. In addition, income in money has increased. Third, there has been brisk activity in the market. Commodities in the community increased. Fourth, the social order has become more stable. Petty thieves are noticeably absent. What caused these favourable conditions? We believe ... party leadership has been correct.

The First Five-Year Plan, 1952–56

The USSR's financial and technical support

The First Five-Year Plan was closely modelled on Stalin's plans for industry in the USSR. The Soviet model had successfully helped the USSR defeat Germany in the Second World War.

The decision was not only ideological, but practical too. The Soviet Union was China's only major ally. A **grain embargo** imposed by the Western powers as a result of China's involvement in the Korean War (see page 16) meant China had few trading partners and was forced to rely on economic help from the Soviet Union. Later Mao bitterly regretted adopting the Soviet model without adapting it to Chinese circumstances.

In the **Sino-Soviet** Mutual Assistance Treaty of February 1950, China and the Soviet Union had undertaken to 'render the other all possible economic assistance and carry out necessary co-operation'. The Soviet support was extensive and essential. It included a loan of $300 million over five years, help with the construction of iron and steel plants, electric power stations and machinery plants. Eleven thousand experts from the USSR and Communist Eastern Europe were sent to China to provide training, advice and technical help.

The Plan's targets

The target of the Plan was to quickly increase China's heavy industries like coal and steel, constructing advanced industrial plants with modern machines. Mao wanted China to be self-sufficient. In particular, industrial plants could supply the PLA with the modern weapons needed to protect China from the aggression of the West.

The Plan's successes

- China experienced an annual growth rate of over 9 per cent. Most targets set by the Plan were reached or easily surpassed.
- Some spectacular engineering works were undertaken, often for propaganda purposes. These included the massive bridge across the Yangtze River.
- Living standards and job security were both guaranteed.
- The population of towns and cities doubled to over 100 million.
- The CCP established greater control over the people, and provided improved housing, health care and education. Workers were organised into Danwei, which provided permits for welfare, travel and permission to marry.

Table 2.1 The First Five-Year Plan, 1953–57

Indicator	1952 Data	1957 Plan Target	1957 Actual	Percentage of Plan achieved
Coal (*mmt)	68.50	113.00	130.00	115.00
Crude Oil (**tmt)	436.00	2012.00	1458.00	72.50
Steel (mmt)	1.35	4.12	5.35	129.80
Electric Power (billion kwh)	7.26	15.90	19.34	121.60
Locomotives (units)	20.00	200.00	167.00	83.50
Merchant ships (thousand dwt tons)	21.50	179.10	54.00	30.20
Bicycles (thousand units)	80.00	555.00	1174.00	211.50
Trucks (units)	0	4000.00	7500.00	187.50

(*mmt = million metric tons; **tmt = thousand metric tons)

Source: *Communist States in the 20th Century* (Phillips et al): Pearson 2016.

The Plan's failures

- In order to reach output targets, many factories sacrificed quality for quantity, and officials often exaggerated levels of output.
- Most Chinese workers had low levels of literacy and basic skills, which held back economic growth in the short and long term.
- China's administrators lacked organisational and managerial experience. This led to a lack of co-operation between industries and central planners, often causing bottlenecks in production.

Simple essay style

Below is a sample exam question. Use your own knowledge and the information on the opposite page to produce a plan for this question. Choose four general points and provide three pieces of specific information to support each general point. Once you have planned your essay, write the introduction and conclusion for the essay. The introduction should list the points to be discussed in the essay. The conclusion should summarise the key points and justify which point was the most important.

How accurate is it to say that the First Five-Year Plan transformed the Chinese economy?

The flaw in the argument

Below is a sample exam question and a paragraph written in answer to this question. The paragraph contains an argument which attempts to answer the question. However, there is an error in the argument. Use your knowledge of this topic to identify the flaw in the argument.

'The First Five-Year Plan was an undeniable success.' How far do you agree with this statement?

In conclusion, this statement is unquestionably correct. The First Five-Year Plan was a great success because it stimulated unprecedented improvement in Chinese industrial production. Badly damaged by the Civil War and the Second World War, industry in China was devastated but the Five-Year Plan completely revived it. The biggest beneficiaries were the urban workers. For the first time, they could be assured of stable and secure work all the year round. Their standard of living increased and consumer goods flooded the shops. Finally, the plan was a great success for the Communist Party: after years of being embarrassed as a backward nation, the First Five-Year Plan showed that Communism could make China a modern, industrial superpower. Therefore, the success of the plan is undeniable.

The Second Five-Year Plan (The Great Leap Forward), 1958–62

Mao's reasons for launching the Second Five-Year Plan

In contrast to the industrial success of the First Five-Year Plan, agricultural production was still low. Mao knew that agriculture needed to become more efficient so that it could feed the urban workers who were building China's modern factories. China did not have much technology, but what Mao could call upon was manpower – some 600 million people. Dismissive of experts and intellectuals, he believed in mass mobilisation: that if people worked together with a revolutionary spirit, with great strength of will, any target could be attained, any obstacle overcome. Even if he had wanted to rely on orthodox economic planning, there were few experts left after the Anti-Rightist campaign to advise him or to warn against his folly. He had no choice but to rely on mass mobilisation to increase production. Mao had good reason to feel confident that his policy would be a success:

- Mao was desperate to transform China into a great economic power. He also wanted to place China as the leading Communist nation in Asia. In 1957, the Soviet leader, Nikita Khrushchev, made a dramatic speech in which he promised that the USSR would overtake the United States in industrial production by 1980. Not to be outdone, Mao told the Party that 'We must start a technological revolution so that we may overtake Britain in fifteen or more years.' Mao wanted to show that he could make China strong by following a specifically Chinese path, independent of the Soviet Union.
- Although agriculture had faltered, industrial production had risen dramatically during the First Five-Year Plan. This success had convinced him that very rapid and very large improvements in agricultural production could be made.
- Mao's optimism was further enhanced because it appeared that the Communists were winning the **Cold War**. Communist technology appeared more advanced than that of the West: with the launching of Sputnik, in 1957, the **space race** looked won. In a speech in Moscow in 1957, a confident Mao declared that 'The East wind is prevailing over the West wind.'
- Mao wanted to achieve what was termed 'Walking on Two Legs': increasing both agricultural and industrial production at the same time. The regime declared that 'General Steel' and 'General Grain' were in charge of the economy.
- As a result of the Anti-Rightist campaign, there were no longer any opponents who would openly disagree with Mao's political policies. Everyone in the Party knew that the best way to advance their careers would be to agree with Mao. There were no experts left to disagree, challenge or even suggest alternative, more logical policies.

State-owned enterprises

During the Great Leap Forward, industrial firms were taken over to create state-owned enterprises. The Party dictated the prices the businesses could charge and the production targets that they had to meet, theoretically for the good of the nation, not for profit. Wages were set by the Party at a guaranteed level. Workers were given a home as well as health care and education. This meant that the enterprises were inefficient: it did not matter how much effort a worker put in, he was still paid the same and had very little incentive to be productive. Managers were not rewarded for being efficient either: any surplus they produced was taken away by the state anyway.

 Mind map

Use the information on the opposite page to add detail to the mind map below.

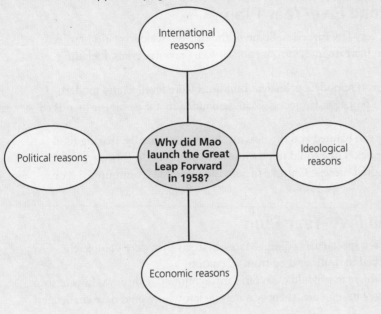

International reasons

Political reasons

Why did Mao launch the Great Leap Forward in 1958?

Ideological reasons

Economic reasons

 Develop the detail

Below are a sample exam-style question and a paragraph written in answer to this question. The paragraph contains a limited amount of detail. Annotate the paragraph to add additional detail to the answer.

How accurate is it to say that Mao's ambitions for the Second Five-Year Plan were hopelessly unrealistic?

Mao believed that the Chinese workers were capable of creating an advanced economy which would overtake Britain in fifteen years. He was convinced that this would be achieved largely by the mass mobilisation of millions of people. He believed that China could easily build on the achievements of the First Five-Year Plan.

Successes and failures of the Second Five-Year Plan, 1958–62

Successes of the Second Five-Year Plan

- The Great Leap Forward had very few successes. Some of the smaller-scale irrigation projects were of value and there was an increase in the production of some raw materials, including steel and oil.
- Tiananmen Square in Beijing was remodelled: ancient buildings were levelled and modern new buildings erected. It was a propaganda success: Mao demanded that it be bigger than Red Square in Moscow.
- Ideologically, private property was banned and the peasants lived communally, sharing food halls and parenting responsibilities. They could not own private property. In this way, one could see the plan as an ideological success: Chinese society did resemble Communism more closely than before.

Failures of the Second Five-Year Plan

- The Second Five-Year Plan was a spectacular failure. Mao set targets that were completely unrealistic. Millions were worked to death or died from starvation.
- His belief that mobilisation of the masses could overcome any economic reality was hopelessly optimistic and with the purges of his enemies there was no one left who would dare challenge him openly.
- Huge projects like the Three-Gate Gorge dam over the Yellow River were so badly planned they caused environmental damage that made farming more difficult. Foreign visitors were banned from seeing it in case they spread unfavourable rumours when they returned home.
- Desperate to increase steel production, he demanded that the people build home-made 'backyard furnaces' (see textbox below). Factories had to close for lack of raw materials. By 1962, industrial production had declined by 40 per cent from the 1958–59 level.

Backyard furnaces

Mao believed that one way to increase steel production would be to demand that peasants make home-made furnaces. Party cadres, desperate to meet the unrealistic production targets, demanded that the peasants work around the clock to keep the furnaces working. When normal fuel was used up, the peasants were compelled to put cooking implements like woks, as well as chairs, tables, doors and even the roofs of the houses into the furnace. Predictably, the steel produced was of such poor quality that it was useless. Meanwhile, crops rotted in the fields while peasants tended the furnaces and many died of malnutrition or exhaustion.

Table 2.2 Economic results of the Great Leap Forward, 1957–62

Year	Grain (million tonnes)	Steel (million tonnes)	Oil (million tonnes)	Coal (million tonnes)
1957	195.1	5.4	1.5	131.0
1958	200.0	8.0	2.3	230.0
1959	170.0	10.0	3.7	290.0
1960	143.5	13.0	4.5	270.0
1961	147.5	8.0	4.5	180.0
1962	160.0	8.0	5.3	180.0

Michael Lynch, *Access to History: The People's Republic of China, 1949–76*, second edition (2008)

Quick quizzes at **www.hoddereducation.co.uk/myrevisionnotes**

Write the question

The following sources relate to the Great Leap Forward. Read the guidance detailing what you need to know about the Great Leap Forward during this period. Having done this, write an exam-style question using the sources.

_____

_____

SOURCE 1

From Jung Chang, Wild Swans, *1992. The source is from a memoir that describes life as a woman during Mao's rule. Her family were Party cadres. She was six years old at the start of the Great Leap Forward. The failure of Mao's policies led her to leave China and live in the West.*

Agriculture was also neglected because of the priority given to steel. Many of the peasants were exhausted from having to spend long hours finding fuel, scrap iron and iron ore and keeping the furnaces going. The fields were often left to the women and children, who had to do everything by hand, as the animals were busy making their contribution to steel production. When harvest time came in autumn 1958, few people were in the fields. The failure to get in the harvest in 1958 flashed a warning that a food shortage was on its way, even though official statistics showed a double-digit increase in agricultural output. It was officially announced that in 1958 China's wheat output had overtaken that of the United States. The Party newspaper, the People's Daily, started a discussion on the topic 'How do we cope with the problem of producing too much food?'

SOURCE 2

'More on the Question of Setting up Urban People's Communes'. Newspaper article, 19 January 1959.

It is conceivable that in the not distant future our cities will become area in which several big factories form the backbone, where workers, peasants, traders, students, and soldiers are closely combined, and complete facilities are available for cultural, educational, and welfare work. By that time, the cities will have been built like an orchard with green fields and forests separating one industrial area from another, with numerous small cities lying hidden in the green sea like small islands. One city area alone will have clear creeks, calm lakes, rows of buildings separated by fruit trees and flowers, broad streets and wide paths. Busy markets are in the depth of orchards and orchards are near busy markets. This is a picture of the new socialist and Communist cities we are now building.

 Recommended reading

- J. Becker, *Hungry Ghosts: Mao's Secret Famine* (Griffin, 1998)
- F. Dikotter, *Mao's Great Famine* (Bloomsbury, 2010)
- J. Yang, *Tombstone: The Great Chinese Famine, 1958–62* (Penguin, 2008)

The Lushan Conference, 1959

In July 1959, the Party held a conference at the mountain town of Lushan in Jiangxi. Minister of Defence Peng Duhuai voiced doubts about the reports of a record grain harvest (375 million tons). Peng, a former peasant, had travelled to his home village in Hunan province and had witnessed the plight of the peasantry; he wrote a private letter to Mao in which he raised the issue of exaggerated reporting. He believed that his status in the Party would protect him. He had long been a close colleague of Mao's, a brilliant military leader, a hero of the struggle against the Nationalists and of the Korean War. However, Mao felt betrayed. He made Peng's letter public and accused Peng of colluding with Soviet leader Nikita Khrushchev behind his back. Peng was replaced by a devoted ally of Mao, **Lin Biao**. This sent a message to the Party: no criticism of Mao was possible.

Liu, Deng and economic reform, 1962–65.

Although Mao claimed that the weather was the main cause of the failures of the Great Leap Forward, he was forced to take a step back from the day-to-day running of the country. Instead, Liu and Deng introduced economic reforms. They were pragmatists: as Deng famously said, 'It doesn't matter if a cat is black or white, so long as it catches mice.'

The reforms were successful to a large extent:

- In industry, factories were told to make a profit, instead of aiming for Communist ideology.
- Factories were told to make products to help agriculture like steel, wood and bamboo to make tools, carts and boats.
- By 1965, industrial output was nearly double that recorded in 1957.
- Light industry such as clothes and furniture grew at a rate of 27 per cent each year.
- Heavy industry was growing at a rate of 17 per cent.
- Experts who had been sent to the Laogai during the Anti-Rightist campaign were released and returned to management posts.
- By the end of 1962, the availability of tools, boats and carts had been restored to the same level as before the introduction of communes.
- The communes were reduced in size and the peasants given greater freedom to grow what they wanted and to sell the surplus for profit at market.
- The opportunity to work private plots provided an incentive for the harder-working, more experienced and entrepreneurial peasants to improve their lives: they grasped this chance and by the mid-1960s private production accounted for approximately one-third of peasants' incomes.

Explain the difference

The following sources give different accounts of the effects of the Great Leap Forward. List the ways in which the sources differ. Explain the differences between the sources using their provenance (at the top of each source) and the historical context. Make sure you stay focused on the differences that are relevant to the question.

How far could the historian make use of Sources 1 and 2 together to investigate the effects of the Great Leap Forward? Explain your answer, using both sources, the information given about them and your own knowledge of the historical context.

SOURCE 1

From a letter from Peng Dehuai to Mao Zedong, 1959.

Dear Chairman:

The Lushan meeting is important. Please consider whether what I am about to write is worth your attention, point out whatever is wrong and give me your instructions. The Great Leap Forward has basically proved the correctness of the General Line for building socialism with greater, quicker, better, and more economical results in a country like ours. But as we can see now, an excessive number of capital construction projects were hastily started in 1958. With part of the funds being dispersed, completion of some essential projects had to be postponed. This is a shortcoming, one caused mainly by lack of experience. So we continued with our Great Leap Forward in 1959 instead of putting on our brakes and slowing down our pace accordingly. As a result, imbalances were not corrected in time. In the nationwide campaign for the production of iron and steel, too many small blast furnaces were built with a waste of material, money, and manpower. This is, of course, a rather big loss. On the other hand, through the campaign we have been able to conduct a preliminary geological survey across the country, train many technicians, temper the vast numbers of cadres and raise their level. The exaggeration trend has become so common in various areas and departments that reports of unbelievable miracles have appeared to bring a great loss of prestige to the Party. Extravagance and waste grew in the wake of reports of extra-large grain and cotton harvests and a doubling of iron and steel output. As a result, the autumn harvest was done in a slipshod manner, and costs were not taken into consideration. Though we were poor, we lived as if we were rich.

SOURCE 2

From a speech by Mao made at Chengchow, February 27, 1959.

In 1958, we achieved great successes on every front. On the ideological and political front, the industrial front, the agricultural front … matter where, it was the same in all. Especially remarkable was that the fact that there was a magnificent leap forward in the area of industrial and agricultural production. In a new and historically unprecedented social movement that involves several hundred million people and for which previous experience is lacking, like the setting up of the people's communes, both the people and their leaders can only acquire experience step by step. Anyone who says that a broad social movement can be completely without shortcomings is nothing but a dreamer … or simply a hostile element. As for the relationship between our achievement and defects, it is, just as we have often said, like the relationship between nine of the ten fingers, and the one remaining finger. There are some people who doubt or deny the achievements of the Great Leap Forward of 1958. This kind of viewpoint is completely mistaken.

Exam focus

Below is a sample answer to the following exam-style question. Read the answer and the comments around it. Bear these in mind when tackling the activity at the end.

'Mao's policies were entirely to blame for the Great Famine of 1958–62.' How far do you agree with this statement?

This statement is correct to a great extent. The Great Leap Forward was an attempt to increase Chinese agricultural and industrial production very rapidly. It was a complete failure which cost the lives of over 30 million Chinese. It was Mao who decided to launch the Great Leap Forward that led to the famine. It was his policies that created a political environment which made famine more likely. It is clear that without Mao's policies there would not have been a famine. However, he is not entirely to blame. The Party cadres lied to Mao about the true levels of production, and the weather exacerbated the famine.

> The introduction is directed and focused. It suggests the way in which the answer will develop, and notes some of the wider factors at work in the period.

Mao's policies were greatly responsible for the famine. It was Mao's belief in the idea of 'Walking on Two Legs' that meant that China attempted to increase production in agriculture and industry simultaneously. This was far too ambitious and frantic, a poorly planned economic development that created unrealistic targets for production. Mao's belief in 'mass mobilisation' – that through sheer force of will and hard work any economic obstacle could be overcome – meant that he refused to listen to his colleagues like Liu Shaoqi and Deng Xiaioping who advised him to adopt a more pragmatic approach. One example of his misguided policies was steel production. He demanded that peasants create 'backyard furnaces', small steel-producing furnaces. He demanded incredibly high production from the furnaces and this led peasants to burn vital fuel, including cooking fuel, and to melt down their cooking utensils and woks. Unable to cook food, many died of starvation. Furthermore, they could not take time to collect the harvest. Others were simply too exhausted by trying to keep up with Mao's production targets to be able to collect the harvest. Food rotted in the fields while the people starved.

> The answer discusses the stated factor of Mao's policies, and explains the devastating effect they had in the countryside.

Mao's economic plan to create self-sufficient communes also contributed to the famine. In the communes, peasants would live collectively, sharing everything: land, food and even parenting responsibilities. The high production targets meant that time spent by peasants doing anything other than working had to be reduced. Mao introduced food halls: these were meant to reduce the burden on women of cooking food. However, they were extremely badly supplied. Soon the food ran out but with woks and oil allocated to the backyard furnaces, people were no longer able to cook for themselves. Women were forced to turn to prostitution to survive, while many men were forced to leave their families to forage for food.

> The role of the communes in the famine is addressed. While the information here is accurate, the material is focused on the social impact of the communes rather than on the famine itself.

Mao had a personal, political objective in the launching of the Great Leap Forward for industry and agriculture. He wanted to make himself the key leader of Communism in Asia, above the leader of the Soviet Union. He wanted to be able to boast that his economic policies were more successful than those of the Soviet Union. It was his personal desire to impress the Soviets that gave rise to his overly ambitious economic policy and thus the Great Famine: even when it was clear that the Great Leap Forward was a failure, he refused to back down and continued to export food to the USSR.

> The information in this paragraph is not strongly linked to the famine, which is only mentioned briefly at the end.

However, Mao cannot take the entire blame for the devastating famine of 1958–62. The Party cadres must also take some blame. Desperate to advance their careers, they exaggerated the success of the Great Leap Forward, making ridiculous claims about the level of food being harvested. Fooled into believing that production targets were being met, Mao kept increasing the target, leading to ever-greater food requisitioning and even more widespread starvation. However, Mao should still take most of the blame. His use of violent campaigns such as the Three and Five Antis campaigns had created an atmosphere of terror where no one was willing to speak out against his policies. Anyone who might have offered criticism of his economic policies or suggested more rational and pragmatic policies had been silenced. They remembered the Hundred Flowers campaign: no one was willing to speak up any more. His purging of opponents within the Party, such as Gao Gang and Rao Shushi in 1954, meant that no other Party leaders were willing to point out the problems of Mao's policies. By 1958, Mao was surrounded by advisers who were too scared to do anything other than agree with him.

The answer investigates some other reasons for the famine, with some good references to exaggerated figures on agricultural output and to the widespread culture of fear which prevented people from speaking out about the famine.

Finally, an important reason for the severity of the famine was that the weather was particularly bad. Typhoons caused flooding in South China and there were droughts that reduced the flow of the Yellow River by two-thirds. Eight of the twelve main rivers in Shandong province dried up. Over 2 million people died through drowning or because their crops were destroyed. Mao himself believed that weather conditions had caused the famine and it is true that the weather in 1958 did reduce the harvest.

In conclusion, it is clear that Mao's economic policies did contribute to the severity of the famine of 1958–62, but they were not the only reason. Mao's use of terror in the preceding years meant that no one was willing to argue with him. Also, ambitious Party cadres conspired to falsify their production levels, causing Mao to impose ever-greater targets. Furthermore, the weather conditions in this period were an important contributing factor. Overall, however, the failure of Mao's policies was the greatest factor. It was Mao's over-ambitious economic targets that produced a political environment with the incentive to lie about production levels. It was Mao's personal desire for prestige and power that led him to try to increase production so rapidly. Although weather conditions did contribute to the failure of the Great Leap Forward in the first year, Mao was wrong to claim that they were the biggest factor. The weather improved after 1958 and so weather conditions can only be seen as a contributing factor that exacerbated the problems of the Leap, rather than a fundamental cause. In the final analysis, Mao must take by far the greatest responsibility for the devastating famine of 1958–62.

The conclusion reaches an overall judgement. It makes it clear that there were several reasons for the famine, but that Mao's policies were the most significant factor.

The answer explores a number of key factors and attempts to analyse the relationship between them. There is a good range of accurate factual material deployed, though it is slightly uneven in some places. References to Mao and the USSR are not made very relevant. The conclusion weighs up the relative significance of various factors, and the overall judgement is well substantiated. The organisation of the answer is logical and the argument is clearly made. The answer is a secure Level 4 response.

Changing focus

This essay argues that the most important reason for the Great Famine was Mao's policies, but the essay also considers a range of other factors. Pick one of these other factors and rewrite the introduction, the conclusion and the relevant paragraph, arguing that this factor was the most important.

AS-level question

'Agrarian land reform brought widespread benefits to the people of China.' How far do you agree with this statement?

Mao's reasons for launching the Cultural Revolution `REVISED`

Divisions within the CCP between ideologues and pragmatists

At the end of the Great Leap Forward, Mao had retired to the so-called 'second line', away from day-to-day politics. The Great Leap Forward had been based upon Mao's ideological belief in mass mobilisation, class conflict and trust in the power of revolutionary commitment but this seemed to have failed, leading to the Great Famine. Instead, Liu Shaoqi and Deng Xiaoping had taken control of policy and they advocated a much slower, more pragmatic approach to decision-making. This greatly angered Mao, who believed that the Communist revolution he had worked so long towards was being subverted by opponents who were not ideologically committed enough. The Cultural Revolution was in part an effort to destroy them and return China to his ideologically driven policies.

The quest for permanent revolution

Mao believed that the final creation of a Communist China demanded ongoing revolution. If the people became too comfortable, they would slip back into their old traditions and customs. The people's revolutionary commitment needed to be constantly tested. He believed that every new generation needed to experience revolution. Mao knew that many people, including many in the Party, did not remember the struggles of the Civil War. What was needed was another revolution to mobilise the masses and forge them into hardened revolutionaries.

Attacks on the bureaucracy

Mao believed that when bureaucrats stopped working to create revolution, they would become like any other bourgeois ruling class and the government would become corrupt and inefficient like the GMD. Bureaucrats would become comfortable and lazy. They would take advantage of their status to improve their own lives, rewarding themselves with luxuries like houses, cars, food and guaranteed places at the best schools for their children. They would be the new '**Mandarins**'. What was needed was upheaval within the Party, constant struggle with those in authority being replaced by zealous new Communists. The Cultural Revolution was created by Mao to mobilise the masses to purge bourgeois bureaucrats and replace them with those loyal to himself. Mao compared the CCP to a healthy body breathing air and exhaling carbon dioxide. He said 'A **proletarian party** must also get rid of the stale and take in the fresh, for only thus can it be full of vitality.'

Divisions within the CCP between supporters and opponents of Mao's policies

Mao's supporters

The CCP was divided over Mao's ideological outlook. Mao did have some very committed supporters like **Chen Boda**, his chief of propaganda, **Kang Sheng**, his chief of secret police, **Jiang Qing**, and Lin Biao, the head of the PLA. They provided vital support in his plan to purge his rivals. They were part of the **Central Cultural Revolution Group (CCRG)**, a subcommittee within the Politburo. They believed that the government and Party had become 'bureaucratised' and a campaign was needed to remove counter-revolutionary opponents and replace them with fervent, committed radicals.

Mao's opponents

There were pragmatists within the Party who were committed Communists but who wanted a more rational, pragmatic approach to creating Communism. They believed that the Great Leap Forward had failed in part because it had been too radical and ambitious. The most important of these were Liu and Deng. Economic planners like Chen Yun and Bo Yibo argued that experts and intellectuals were needed to help run the economy. Mao could not simply remove his enemies: they were popular among the people and the Party. Instead, Mao used the Cultural Revolution as a means to attack his enemies. The play *Hai Rui Dismissed from Office* told of a Ming dynasty official who was dismissed for criticising the Emperor. Mao and his allies believed that this was a veiled criticism of Mao's treatment of Peng Dehuai. The decision to allow its publication was made by Peng Zhen, the mayor of Beijing. He was criticised and forced to resign. He was a good friend of Liu and Deng. When he was removed, it made it easier for Mao to attack Liu and Deng.

! Spot the mistake

Below is a sample exam-style question and a paragraph written in answer to this question. Why does this paragraph not get into Level 5? Once you have identified the mistake, rewrite the paragraph so that it displays the qualities of Level 5. The mark scheme on page 82 will help you.

'Mao launched the Cultural Revolution as a means to remove his political opponents.' How far do you agree with this judgement?

Mao launched the Cultural Revolution because he wanted to get rid of his opponents. Mao believed that the Party was no longer the force for revolutionary change that he had led into power in 1949. Instead of order and stability, he demanded 'permanent revolution'. Mao feared that the Party had become bureaucratised. He believed that after it had taken power in the revolution, some cadres had exploited their new power for their own advantage. After removing China's old rulers, they had become a new elite, taking advantage of the masses and living a life of luxury with better houses, cars, food and guaranteed access to the best schools for their children. The only way to prevent this was for revolution to be permanent, to regularly replace those in authority to prevent them from ever becoming comfortable and secure. Therefore it is clear that Mao launched the Cultural Revolution to remove his opponents.

⦿ Spot the inference

High-level answers avoid excessive summarising or paraphrasing of the sources. They instead make inferences from the sources, as well as analysing their value in terms of their context. Below is a source and a series of statements. Read the source and decide which of the statements:

- make inferences from the source (I)
- paraphrase the source (P)
- summarise the source (S)
- cannot be justified from the source (X).

Statement	I	P	S	X
The need for class conflict was ongoing.				
The Cultural Revolution was a way to attack Mao's opponents like Liu and Deng.				
Violence and anarchy are a necessary part of revolution.				
The old bourgeois class was still trying to control China and had to be overthrown by violent action.				

SOURCE 1

'The 16 Points: Guidelines for the Great Proletarian Cultural Revolution', quoted in Mark Selden (ed.) The People's Republic of China: A Documentary History of Revolutionary Change (1979), pages 549–56.

Although the bourgeoisie has been overthrown, it is still trying to use the old ideas, culture, customs and habits of the exploiting classes to corrupt the masses, capture their minds and endeavour to stage a comeback. At present, our objective is to struggle against and overthrow those persons in authority who are taking the capitalist road, to criticise and repudiate the reactionary bourgeoisie academic 'authorities' and the ideology of the bourgeoisie and all other exploiting classes and to transform education, literature and art ... In the great proletarian Cultural Revolution, the only method is for the masses to liberate themselves ... Don't be afraid of disturbances. Chairman Mao has often told us that revolution cannot be so very refined, so gentle, so temperate, kind, courteous, restrained and magnanimous. Let the masses educate themselves. It is imperative to hold aloft the great banner of Mao Zedong's Thought. Mao Zedong Thought should be taken as the guide for action ... Party committees at all levels must abide by the directions given by Chairman Mao.

Mao's hold on young people

In order to seize back power from the 'capitalist roaders', Mao realised that he needed to mobilise the young people of China to support him. He knew that they did not remember the worst of the Great Famine and did not blame him for it. In school they had learned that he was a great hero who had defeated the Nationalists, given land to the peasants and stood up to the Americans in the Korean War. This indoctrination meant that he could easily control them. They read the **Little Red Book** (see textbox below) and believed the cult of personality that portrayed him as a God who could never be wrong. When he wrote a **Big Character Poster** that called on them to 'Bombard the Headquarters' and attack the pragmatists within the CCP, they obeyed.

The Little Red Book

In 1964, the head of the PLA, Lin Biao, commissioned the publication of a collection of Mao's most famous statements. He ordered every soldier to read it and learn to adhere to its every instruction. Soon it was not only the army that was reading the book: the young people in the Red Guards, who had been taught at school to revere Mao, also tried to decipher and follow its ideas, which took on a near-religious power. Some believed that it could work miracles. Newspapers reported that doctors with the book had cured blind people. One disabled person declared that learning Mao Zedong Thought had enabled him to walk again. There was even a report that reading quotations from the book had raised a man from the dead.

The mass rallies of 1966

In August 1966, Mao and Chen Boda invited millions of students to attend a series of mass rallies in Beijing. PLA Chief Lin Biao helped organise the transportation of the students to the capital. Ecstatic at seeing their hero in person, Mao whipped them into a revolutionary fervour. Mao told them that they had a special role to play: 'The world belongs to you', he said, 'China's future belongs to you'. China had always been a hierarchical society: Confucian Thought, taught in schools, told children to be obedient to their parents and not question authority. Now Mao encouraged them to 'Dare to rebel against authority', a veiled suggestion that they attack all symbols of authority like teachers and government officials, and even his enemies within the Party leadership like Liu and Deng.

The Red Guards' attacks on the 'Four Olds'

Mao encouraged the young people who idolised him to join the Red Guards, groups of violent youngsters totally dedicated to Mao. In August 1966, he launched the 'Four Olds' campaign, urging the Red Guards to attack 'old ideas', 'old culture', 'old customs' and 'old habits'. The 'olds', he said, were still used by the **bourgeois feudal classes** to repress the Chinese people. Religious buildings were destroyed and anyone who owned classical literature or music could be attacked. Religious ideas like Confucianism and ancestor worship were condemned. These 'old' ideas needed to be destroyed and replaced by 'new' Communist ideology. Shop signs were changed to read 'Defend Mao Zedong' or 'Permanent Revolution'. Children's names were changed to 'Red Glory' or 'Face the East'. Road signs were altered – the British embassy now stood on 'Anti-Imperialism Road'.

Add the context

Below is a sample exam question with the accompanying Sources. Having read the question and the sources, complete the following activity.

> How far could the historian make use of Sources 1 and 2 together to investigate the impact of the Red Guards?

First, look for aspects of each source that refer to the events and discussion that were going on around the time that the source was written. Underline the key phrases and write a brief description of the context in the margin next to the source. Draw an arrow from the key phrase to the context. Try and find three key phrases in each source.

Tip: Your contextual knowledge may not always support the information in the source. You could also consider ways in which your knowledge of context can be used to challenge the account of the source. In cases such as these, consider how the provenance of the source may have had an impact on its accuracy.

SOURCE 1

From Nien Cheng, Life and Death in Shanghai, *1986. The author of this autobiography was arrested and imprisoned for six years during the Cultural Revolution.*

In the days after Mao reviewed the first group of Red Guards in Beijing, and gave them his blessing, the Red Guards in Shanghai took over the streets. The newspaper announced that the mission of the Red Guards was to rid the country of the 'Four Olds'. There was no clear definition of 'old'; it was left to the Red Guards to decide. First of all they changed street names. The main thoroughfare of Shanghai along the waterfront, the Bund, was renamed Revolution Boulevard. They smashed flower and curio shops because, they said, only the rich had the money to spend on such frivolities. The other shops were examined and goods they considered offensive or unsuitable for a socialist society they destroyed or confiscated. Because they did not think a socialist man should sit on a sofa, all sofas became taboo.

SOURCE 2

This source is from a document written by Mao and published in the People's Daily. *The term 'white terror' was used to describe counter-revolutionary opposition to the Cultural Revolution.*

Bombard the Headquarters, 5 August 1966.

China's first Marxist-Leninist big character poster and commentator's article on it in the People's Daily are indeed superbly written! Comrades, please read them again. But in the last fifty days or so some leading comrades from the central down to the local levels have acted in a diametrically opposite way. Having the reactionary stand of the bourgeoisie, they have enforced a bourgeois dictatorship and struck down the surging movement of the Great Cultural Revolution of the Proletariat. They have stood facts on their heads and juggled black and white, encircled and repressed revolutionaries, stifled opinions differing from their own, imposed a white terror, and felt very pleased with themselves. They have puffed up the arrogance of the bourgeoisie and deflated the morale of the proletariat.

 Recommended reading

- Jung Chang, *Wild Swans: Three daughters of China*, pages 362–572 (Harper Collins, 1993)
- Han Suyin, *Wind in the Tower*, pages 205–305 (Jonathan Cape, 1976)
- Ji-Li Jiang, *Red Scarf Girl: A memoir of the Cultural Revolution* (Harper Collins, 2010)
- Gao Yuan, *Born Red: A chronicle of the Cultural Revolution* (Stanford University Press, 1987)
- Nien Cheng, *Life and Death in Shanghai* (Grafton, 1989)

Following Mao's demand to 'Smash the Four Olds' the Red Guards got out of hand. They attacked figures of authority, forcing them to make self-denunciations at struggle meetings. Others were tortured and murdered. At first, young people who had a bourgeois background were not allowed to join the Red Guards. When this restriction was lifted, these members of the so-called 'black elements' were desperate to prove their revolutionary credentials, committing brutal crimes to show how loyal to Mao they were. This period was known as 'the Terror'. It was not just motivated by ideology. Many young people were violent because of peer pressure. Others wanted to remove rivals for career advancement. There was anarchy when rival bands of Red Guards from different schools and colleges competed to prove that they were the most ideologically committed. Those Red Guards who were from working-class families fought against Red Guards who were middle class. Factories might have two different Red Guard factions.

The use of terror

The anarchy threatened to get out of hand. Much of the blame should go to Mao himself. In the so-called 'January Storm' of 1967, Red Guards seized power from the CCP itself and set up a government modelled on the 1871 Paris Commune. This was a step too far for Mao and he used the PLA to close down the commune. Fearing that the chaos would spread into its own ranks, the PLA now acted to crush radicals across China. This time Mao sided with the radicals and denounced the crackdown as the **'February Adverse Current'**, encouraging the radicals to greater violence. Finally, just as full-scale civil war looked likely, Mao realised that the chaos meant that China might be vulnerable to attack from foreign nations and acted. He used the PLA to once again restore order.

Why did young people join the Red Guards?

The Revolution offered various opportunities to youths. The Party ruled that anyone wearing the armband denoting them to be a member of the Red Guards would be allowed to board a train for free without buying a ticket if they supported Mao. Many young people travelled to Beijing to cheer on Mao at vast rallies in Tiananmen Square, or visit the places that Mao had lived while he was fighting the Civil War against the Nationalists. Others simply took the chance, after years of control and repression, to travel across the country, moved more by curiosity and the opportunity to experience freedom as much as revolutionary zeal. While some were committed enough to participate in the torture and intimidation of those denounced as 'class enemies', others simply chanted slogans and attended the rallies out of peer pressure.

Cultural destruction

Cultural objects related to the 'Four Olds' were attacked by hordes of Red Guards. Sculptures, statues and artefacts were defaced and desecrated. Libraries with Western books or traditional literature were burned. Temples, like the temple to Confucius in Shandong, were ransacked and priceless cultural relics destroyed. Buddhist relics were attacked and in Tibet any aspect of Buddhist culture was destroyed. Nineteenth-century cultural hero Wu Xun had his corpse exhumed by middle-school students, who walked with it to a public square, broke it up into little pieces and burned it. The treasures of the Forbidden City were only saved when Zhou Enlai sent the PLA to protect it from the Red Guards.

Support or challenge?

Below is a sample exam question which asks how far you agree with a specific statement. Below this is a series of general statements which are relevant to the question. Using your own knowledge and the information on the opposite page, decide whether these statements support or challenge the statement in the question and tick the appropriate box.

'Genuine commitment to Maoist ideology was the most important reason people joined the Red Guards.' How far do you agree with this argument?

Statement	Support	Challenge
Young people were indoctrinated to support Mao in schools.		
Many young people joined the Red Guards because of peer pressure.		
Millions of young people followed Mao's call to attack the 'Four Olds'.		
Joining the Red Guards gave young people a chance to travel.		
China was a very hierarchical society and young people were taught to be subservient to their elders.		
Red Guards competed to prove how ideologically committed they were.		
Millions of young people obeyed Mao's call for mass mobilisation against his enemies.		
Young people took the chance to take revenge against teachers who had punished them.		

Complete the paragraph

Below are a sample exam question and a paragraph written in answer to this question. The paragraph contains a point and specific examples, but lacks a concluding analytical link back to the question. Complete the paragraph adding this link in the space provided.

How far do you agree that young people were motivated to join the Red Guards because of Mao's propaganda?

It is correct to say that many young people joined the Red Guards because of Mao's propaganda. They had been taught in school to idolise Mao and were taught that he had almost God-like powers. However, there were other reasons that young people joined the Red Guards. Many joined because of peer pressure from their schoolmates. Furthermore, China had long been a repressive society where young people had few opportunities. Joining the Red Guards encouraged young people to throw off the restraints that controlled them, allowing them to be independent, to travel, to meet new friends, and to fight back against the forces of authority like teachers and older people who they perceived as constraining their freedoms. Overall,

_____

_____

Attacks on Mao's political opponents

Liu Shaoqi

As Head of State, Liu's pragmatic policies had helped rebuild China after the Great Leap Forward. He was popular and Mao may have been jealous. When Mao first encouraged the students to rise up, Liu had supported the sending of Party 'Work Teams' onto the campuses to control the violence. This was used as evidence of his traitorous 'rightist' sentiments. Liu was subjected to constant struggle meetings and he was abused and beaten; his family was also targeted. His wife was publicly denounced and his children sent to the countryside to live as peasants. Liu wrote to Mao begging to be allowed to resign, but Mao did not reply. At the ninth Party Congress, Jiang Qing denounced him as a traitor who had been an agent for the American CIA. The evidence for this had been gathered by Jiang Qing and Kang Sheng, who had tortured prisoners to get it. Denounced as a 'renegade, scab and traitor' he was stripped of all his posts and replaced by Lin Biao. Liu was exiled from Beijing and, in time, torture and neglect meant he could no longer speak. He died on 12 November 1968 and was buried in an unmarked grave.

Deng Xiaoping

Mao was also angered by Deng Xiaoping. His famous dictum about the irrelevance of the 'colour' of a policy was a direct affront to Mao's belief that it was better to be Communist than practical. Deng had helped Liu introduce economic reforms without Mao's advice. Mao complained, 'Deng Xiaoping never came to consult me … from 1959 to the present he has never consulted me over anything at all.' Damned as 'the number two person in authority taking the capitalist road', he was accused of trying to establish his own 'Independent Kingdom'. Deng disappeared from public sight, having been sent to a tractor factory in rural Jiangxi. Deng's family also suffered: his son attempted to escape torture by jumping out of a window (some say he was pushed by Red Guards) and was paralysed from the waist down. Deng was later returned to power by Mao, who needed him to help end the chaos of the Cultural Revolution. He was a target of radicals and so was blamed for the protests that followed the death of Zhou Enlai. The **Gang of Four** radicals blamed Deng for the violent clashes with police during the 1976 Qingming festival.

The Gang of Four convinced Mao to take away Deng's positions of government leadership. However, after the death of Mao, Deng eventually became the most important leader in the PRC (see page 54 for details).

Lin Biao and the role of the PLA

Lin Biao was Mao's most subservient follower, whose loyalty had impressed Mao so much that he was chosen to replace the disgraced Peng Dehuai after the Lushan meeting. Lin had also helped create the Little Red Book that helped spread Mao's cult of personality. Lin wrote a foreword to the book that lauded Mao as practically a deity; it was made compulsory reading for PLA soldiers. It demanded self-sacrifice in the service of the Chairman and was distributed to millions of soldiers. The PLA newspaper began to publish a quotation from Mao every day. Soldiers were ordered to cut them out and compile their own collections of Mao's quotes to be studied and recited. The cult of **Lei Feng** encouraged obedience to Mao Zedong Thought (see textbox below). When the violence of the Cultural Revolution spiralled out of control, Mao was able to rely on the complete loyalty of the PLA to control it.

'Learn from the PLA'

The 'Learn from the PLA' campaign was launched in 1963. Army propaganda turned one rank-and-file soldier, Lei Feng, into an ideological role model and a national hero. Described in Party propaganda as 'one of Chairman Mao's good warriors', Lei was a soldier who was deeply loyal to the Party and Mao. Posters showed him digging wells for peasants and helping old ladies to cross the road. Mao declared, 'Be like Comrade Lei Feng', exhorting people to follow his example of revolutionary zeal and loyalty to the leader. When he died in an accident while on duty, his diary was published. It recalled his service to his comrades and also showed him to be unselfish in the service of the revolution. For example, on a train he would help the staff clean the carriages and in the barracks he would secretly mend his comrades' clothes. The myth of Lei Feng helped create loyalty to Mao.

Eliminate irrelevance

Below are a sample exam question and a paragraph written in answer to this question. Read the paragraph and identify parts of the paragraph that are not directly relevant to the question. Draw a line through the information that is irrelevant and justify your deletions in the margin.

> How accurate is it to say the support of the PLA was the most important factor in Mao's defeat of his political opponents during Cultural Revolution?

The PLA was clearly vitally important in Mao's defeat of his opponents during the Cultural Revolution. The PLA was an important tool by which Mao consolidated his control of China. They defeated his opponents during the rectification campaigns in Tibet and Xinjiang. They helped him force the Nationalists into exile to Taiwan, and to build national unity and support for Communism during the Korean War. The PLA helped him during the Cultural Revolution because Mao had the loyalty of PLA leader Lin Biao. Lin published the 'Little Red Book' of Mao's quotations that helped indoctrinate the Red Guards. PLA trucks helped transport the Red Guards to Mao's huge rallies in Beijing. Finally, they helped Mao control the violence of the Cultural Revolution to prevent it getting too far out of hand. However, Mao's political opponents were not all defeated: Deng Xiaoping survived and later became ruler of China, introducing capitalist reforms that were the opposite of what Mao would have wanted.

 ## Simple essay style

Below is a sample exam question. Use your own knowledge and the information on the opposite page to produce a plan for this question. Choose four general points and provide three pieces of specific information to support each general point. Once you have planned your essay, write the introduction and conclusion for the essay. The introduction should list the points to be discussed in the essay. The conclusion should summarise the key points and justify which point was the most important.

> How accurate is it to say that the support of political allies was the main reason that Mao defeated his opponents during the Cultural Revolution?

The purging of the CCP membership

When Mao told the people to 'Bombard the Headquarters', he was encouraging them to attack the CCP. He launched a so-called 'rectification campaign' against the CCP to remove any members who had been bourgeois and elitist and replace them with young, fervently revolutionary people. The impact was devastating:

- Up to 70–80 per cent of all Party cadres at regional and provisional level and 60–70 per cent in the organs of central government were purged.
- As many as 14,000 Party cadres were executed as 'traitors' in Yunnan.
- Four out of six of the regional Party First Secretaries and 23 of 29 provincial Party Secretaries were removed.
- Only 9 out of 23 Politburo members survived the purge.
- Two-thirds of the Central Committee were deposed.

Many were sent to undertake 'productive labour and political study', which in reality translated to a life of back-breaking hard labour and indoctrination in the **May Seventh Cadres Schools**. In total, 3 million bureaucrats and cadres were exiled to the countryside. Others were beaten and tortured. An estimated half a million Chinese were killed. The Party First Secretaries of Shanxi and Yunnan committed suicide to escape the torture and intimidation. In 1975, the new Party constitution named Mao Zedong Thought as an official guiding principle of the CCP: Mao had defeated his opponents.

The purging of 'capitalist roaders' and foreigners living in China

The label 'capitalist roader' was used to criticise anyone suspected of not being ideologically committed to Communism and who wanted to take the 'capitalist road' instead. People were interrogated to check that their beliefs were sufficiently revolutionary and their family backgrounds were scrutinised to check if they had any bourgeois family members.

Foreigners in China, particularly those from capitalist or 'imperialist' nations, were attacked. A mob of Red Guards stormed the British embassy in Beijing, staff were attacked and the embassy was set on fire. Mobs lay siege to the French and Soviet embassies, where they set up loudspeakers to broadcast Maoist slogans. The families of Western embassy staff were denied visas to leave China. The Cultural Revolution broke all rules of international diplomacy: in total, citizens of 30 countries were attacked or abused.

Attacks on foreigners

- The Dutch chargé d'affaires was imprisoned in the embassy by a mob for nearly six months.
- Soviet staff who had left the embassy to buy tickets for their families to leave China were trapped in their cars by a mob for 16 hours. Posters were put up at train stations declaring 'Smash Brezhnev's head' (Brezhnev was the Soviet leader after Khrushchev).
- The French trade counsellor was confronted outside his embassy and made to stand in the freezing cold while being denounced for seven hours. The police watched and did nothing to assist him.
- A British journalist, Anthony Grey, was put into solitary confinement for 26 months. Later Red Guards broke into his house and killed his cat!

Identify an argument

Below is a series of definitions, a sample exam-style question and two sample conclusions. One of the conclusions achieves a high level because it contains an argument. The other achieves a lower level because it contains only description and assertion. Identify which is which. The mark scheme on page 82 will help you.

- Description: a detailed account.
- Assertion: a statement of fact or an opinion that is not supported by a reason.
- Reason: a statement that explains or justifies something.
- Argument: an assertion justified with a reason.

How far do you agree that the support of the PLA was the most important reason that Mao defeated his opponents during the Cultural Revolution?

Sample 1

Mao defeated his opponents during the Cultural Revolution. His main opponents were Liu Shaoqi and Deng Xiaoping. They had disagreed with his economic policies and tried to run China in a practical, non-ideological manner. The PLA was very helpful to Mao. It was the biggest army in the world. It had proven itself as a fighting force during the Korean War. The PLA brought young people to the great rallies in Beijing when the crowd had a chance to see their great leader. The PLA were indoctrinated by Maoist propaganda. The Little Red Book, a collection of Mao's statements, was required reading among the soldiers. They read it every day. They also listened to stories about Lei Feng, a soldier completely loyal to Mao. This inspired the PLA to try to emulate Lei Feng and to obey Mao unquestioningly.

Sample 2

The PLA were clearly the most important reason that Mao was able to defeat his opponents during the Cultural Revolution. They were vital in a number of ways. They helped him organise his rallies where he whipped up support for the Red Guards and convinced them to attack his opponents. PLA trucks brought young people to Beijing for the rallies. The PLA were absolutely loyal to Mao. He could use them to control the course of the Cultural Revolution: when it looked like even Mao himself might lose control of the violence and anarchy, he was able to use the PLA to bring order and end the chaos. In the final analysis, the PLA gave Mao a force that he could use to intimidate or destroy his opponents, a vital ally that no one else possessed.

Eliminate irrelevance

Below is a sample exam-style question and a paragraph written in answer to this question. Read the paragraph and identify parts that are not directly relevant to the question. Draw a line through the information that is irrelevant and justify our deletions in the margin.

How far do you agree that the main reason that Mao launched the Cultural Revolution was to destroy his political rivals?

It is clear that Mao launched the Cultural Revolution in large part to destroy his opponents. He was worried that his political rivals like Liu Shaoqi and Deng Xiaoping were trying to take the 'capitalist road' and destroy the progress made by the Communist revolution he had fought most of his life to create. The CCP had become bureaucratic and bourgeois. He removed thousands of Party members. The Party members had lost their revolutionary fervour. They had become elitist, taking advantage of the benefits of being a Party member such as holidays, better food, cars and places at the best schools for their children. Mao wanted to destroy them and return the CCP to being a revolutionary organisation that was genuinely ideologically committed to Communism. Mao wanted to rid China of foreigners: diplomats from other countries were intimidated and attacked. The British embassy was overrun. A number of foreigners were jailed. Getting rid of the foreigners was an important reason why Mao launched the Cultural Revolution.

Restoration of order by the PLA

By 1968, it was clear to Mao that the violence and anarchy he had encouraged was out of control. In August 1967, Mao had declared the purging of capitalist roaders in the PLA to be 'un-strategic'. He was worried that if it continued China would be vulnerable to attack from foreign countries, particularly the USSR, whose Islamic provinces bordered Xingjiang. It was also clear that the economy was suffering from the constant violence and upheaval. To address these issues, Mao sent in the PLA to restore order. The PLA were very happy to do this because they feared that the Red Guards might become too powerful and rival their authority. PLA commanders also feared that the struggle meetings, denunciations and violence might spread into the ranks of the PLA, weakening it as a fighting force. The PLA launched a wave of terror in support of the 'Cleansing of Class Ranks' campaign. Up to 1.84 million people were arrested for allegedly being 'spies', 'bad elements' or 'newly emerged counter-revolutionaries'. Thousands of people were imprisoned, were beaten to death or committed suicide. The PLA restored order to the education system, enabling schools and colleges to reopen after being closed for two years. When the Red Guards protested that a 'black hand' was seeking to suppress them, Mao admitted 'I am the black hand'.

'Up to the mountains and down to the villages' campaign

Mao needed to disband the Red Guards. Eighteen million young guards were sent to 'cool off' in the countryside as part of the 'Up to the mountains and down to the villages' campaign. Mao said that this was to help them understand the importance of manual labour and to realise how important peasants had been to the revolution. In reality, the campaign was organised because it helped Mao restore order: they were sent to remote areas where they could not organise violent actions. It also helped reduce urban unemployment. The young people hated it. They were shocked by how poor the peasants were and how hard they had to work. The peasants resented having to share their meagre food supply with the newcomers, who were inexperienced at manual labour. Many youngsters became disillusioned with Mao, especially when it became clear that those with Party connections or influential families could quickly return to the cities: those without faced the fact that their exile to the countryside was permanent. There was one positive: the **barefoot doctors** initiative (see page 66) helped train paramedics who could care for the peasants. For many in the villages, this was the first modern, trained doctor they had ever met.

Complex essay style

Below is a sample exam-style question, a list of key points to be made in the essay, and a simple introduction and conclusion for the essay. Read the question, the key points and the introduction and conclusion. Rewrite the introduction and the conclusion in order to develop an argument.

How far was the 'up to the mountains and down to the villages' campaign a complete success for China?

Key points

- Some people in remote villages saw a doctor for the first time.
- The villagers resented having to feed and house a new worker.

Introduction

It is not correct to say that the 'Up to the mountains and down to the villages' campaign was a complete success. It did help reduce urban unemployment and improve the lives of the peasants because many of the young people sent to live with them were trained as barefoot doctors: in many cases they were the first modern doctors that the villagers had ever met. However, there were some clear negatives in the campaign. The youngsters hated living in rural poverty: they were shocked at how poor the peasants were. The villagers did not like the newcomers — they consumed scarce food and most of them did not possess any agricultural skills. Most of all, the campaign discredited Mao's image: many young people were angry that they had been sent to the countryside. They resented not being able to return to their normal life and go to schools and colleges.

Conclusion

It is clearly not the case that the 'Up to the mountains and down to the villages' campaign was a complete success...

 You're the examiner

Below is a sample exam-style question and a paragraph written in answer to this question. Read the paragraph and the mark scheme provided on page 82. Decide which level you would award the paragraph. Write the level below, along with a justification for your choice.

'The "Up to the mountains and down to the villages" campaign was a great success.' How far do you agree with this judgement?

Overall, this statement is incorrect: the campaign was not a success, although some did benefit. The young former Red Guards who went into the countryside gained valuable agricultural skills and spread Communist ideology to the peasants in the villages that they stayed in. However, the biggest beneficiary was not the Chinese people, but simply Mao himself. By sending young people away to work on farms, he could reduce urban unemployment. Mao was worried that the Red Guard had caused too much chaos. By sending them out in the countryside, they would not be able to cause trouble. In the long run, the campaign was a failure, even for Mao. The young people sent to the countryside disliked living in the backward conditions in the villages. The villagers did not want to have to feed the new arrivals, who did not have the skills necessary to help. When the young people realised that children of members of the Party could arrange to return to their normal lives, their trust in Mao's promises of equality diminished.

The return to power of Deng Xiaoping and Zhou Enlai

By the early 1970s, Mao's health was failing. Mao clearly had an eye on who would succeed him and was very concerned as to the long-term future of the revolution he had dedicated his life to. He did not trust Jiang Qing, and his chosen successor, Lin Biao, died in bizarre circumstances (see textbox). Mao needed steady and reliable leaders.

The Lin Biao Affair

Lin had been Mao's most trusted servant and was named successor to Mao after Liu was purged. However, Mao began to believe that Lin was plotting to use the PLA to seize power. In 1971, Lin realised that he had lost Mao's trust. Lin decided to flee to the USSR but in his desperation he did not have time to put enough fuel in his plane. It crashed and Lin died. The official explanation that Lin, once lauded as a great hero, was actually a secret enemy spy, was treated with scepticism by the Chinese people. Many no longer trusted what the government, and even Mao himself, told them.

Deng Xiaoping

Mao recalled Deng from his rural exile. Deng was popular and experienced. He used his organisational skills and support within the Party to re-establish order after the Cultural Revolution. He was named as Army Chief of Staff. By 1974, he had regained his post as CCP Secretary.

Zhou Enlai

Zhou was not purged by Mao because he was very useful. Although a pragmatist, he was skilful at avoiding being associated too much with Liu or Deng. He called for the introduction of 'The Four Modernisations': advancement in agriculture, industry, defence and science and technology. Designed to make China a modern world power, the programme called for greater trade links with the West. Less aggressive relations with the West were developed by Zhou when he helped negotiate the visit of American President Richard Nixon to Beijing in 1972. The Four Modernisations were later enacted by Deng Xiaoping.

Reining in the Gang of Four

The Gang of Four

By the mid-1970s, it clear that Mao would soon die. First Liu and then Lin had previously been named as his successor, but with both of them dead, a succession struggle began between radicals and pragmatists. The so-called **Gang of Four** had been part of the CCRG and were radicals that wanted to continue with the Cultural Revolution. They feared that the pragmatists would take over when Mao died. They launched an 'anti-Confucius'

campaign that denounced Lin Biao as a moderate 'rightist'. The real target was not the already-deceased Lin, but others who could be linked to him as fellow moderates, like Zhou and Deng. The campaign failed: people saw through the political motives and could see that it was an attempt by Jiang and her allies to remove their rivals.

By this time, the people were fed up with constant campaigns and upheaval. Just how unpopular the members of the Gang of Four were was made clear by the public reaction to the death of Zhou Enlai in January 1976. When his body was taken to be cremated, a million people lined the streets to pay their respects. In April, during the Qingming festival, where Chinese people pay homage to their dead ancestors, the people of Beijing began laying wreaths at the base of the Monument to the People's Heroes in Tiananmen Square, honouring Zhou Enlai and attacking Jiang Qing and the Gang of Four (see the textbox on this page). When the government sent trucks to remove the wreaths, violence broke out and the riot police had to be sent in to restore order. The Gang of Four blamed Deng and he was again removed from power. Mao now chose the inexperienced and little-known Hua Guofeng as his successor.

> *A poem written on a tribute to Zhou Enlai and placed in Tiananmen Square.*
>
> You must be mad
>
> To want to be an empress
>
> Here's a mirror to look at yourself
>
> And see what you really are.
>
> You've got together a little gang
>
> To stir up trouble all the time,
>
> Hoodwinking the people, capering about.
>
> But your days are numbered…
>
> Quoted in Alan Lawrence, *China under Communism*, page 97 (1998)

The death of Mao, 1976

The Gang of Four believed that it would be easy to undermine Hua Guofeng. On 9 September 1976, Mao died. Hua took over as Party leader and also as Head of State. Knowing that he was vulnerable without Mao, he acted quickly, using the PLA to arrest the Gang of Four. Deng then returned from exile and used his support within the Party to replace Hua. He introduced the Four Modernisations that helped convert China into a 21st-century superpower.

RAG – Rate the timeline

Below is a sample exam-style question and a timeline. Read the question, study the timeline and, using three coloured pens, put a red, amber or green star next to the events to show:

- Red: events and policies that have no relevance to the question.
- Amber: events and policies that have some significance to the question.
- Green: events and policies that are directly relevant to the question.

How far do you agree that Mao defeated his opponents in the Cultural Revolution because of the support of the PLA?

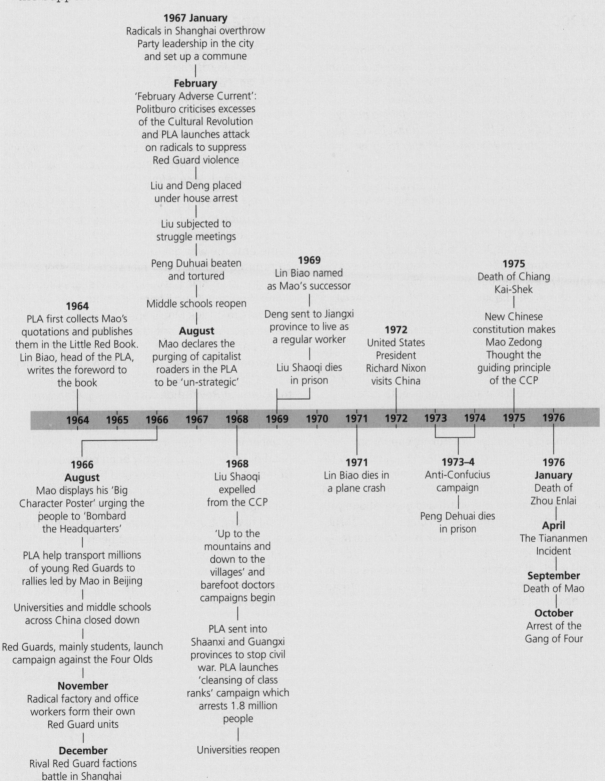

1967 January
Radicals in Shanghai overthrow Party leadership in the city and set up a commune

February
'February Adverse Current': Politburo criticises excesses of the Cultural Revolution and PLA launches attack on radicals to suppress Red Guard violence

Liu and Deng placed under house arrest

Liu subjected to struggle meetings

Peng Duhuai beaten and tortured

Middle schools reopen

1969
Lin Biao named as Mao's successor

Deng sent to Jiangxi province to live as a regular worker

Liu Shaoqi dies in prison

1975
Death of Chiang Kai-Shek

New Chinese constitution makes Mao Zedong Thought the guiding principle of the CCP

1964
PLA first collects Mao's quotations and publishes them in the Little Red Book. Lin Biao, head of the PLA, writes the foreword to the book

August
Mao declares the purging of capitalist roaders in the PLA to be 'un-strategic'

1972
United States President Richard Nixon visits China

Timeline: 1964 1965 1966 1967 1968 1969 1970 1971 1972 1973 1974 1975 1976

1966 August
Mao displays his 'Big Character Poster' urging the people to 'Bombard the Headquarters'

PLA help transport millions of young Red Guards to rallies led by Mao in Beijing

Universities and middle schools across China closed down

Red Guards, mainly students, launch campaign against the Four Olds

November
Radical factory and office workers form their own Red Guard units

December
Rival Red Guard factions battle in Shanghai

1968
Liu Shaoqi expelled from the CCP

'Up to the mountains and down to the villages' and barefoot doctors campaigns begin

PLA sent into Shaanxi and Guangxi provinces to stop civil war. PLA launches 'cleansing of class ranks' campaign which arrests 1.8 million people

Universities reopen

1971
Lin Biao dies in a plane crash

1973–4
Anti-Confucius campaign

Peng Dehuai dies in prison

1976 January
Death of Zhou Enlai

April
The Tiananmen Incident

September
Death of Mao

October
Arrest of the Gang of Four

Exam focus

Below is an exam-style A-level source question and a model answer. Read it and the comments around it.

Study Sources 1 and 2 below before you answer this question.

How far could the historian make use of Sources 1 and 2 together to investigate why Mao launched the Cultural Revolution? Explain your answer, using both sources, the information given about them and your own knowledge of the historical context.

SOURCE 1

Decision of the Central Committee of the Chinese Communist Party Concerning the Great Proletarian Cultural Revolution, 8 August 1966. The Central Committee was an organisation of senior Communist leaders. It was meant to debate policy decisions, but by the time of the Cultural Revolution it was dominated by Mao and met only to agree with his actions.

The Proletarian Cultural Revolution is aimed not only at demolishing all the old ideology and culture and all the old customs and habits, which, fostered by the exploiting classes, have poisoned the minds of the people for thousands of years, but also at creating and fostering among the masses an entirely new ideology and culture and entirely new customs and habits – those of the proletariat. This great task of transforming customs and habits is without any precedent in human history. As for all the classes, the proletarian world outlook must be used to subject them to thoroughgoing criticism. It takes time to clear away the evil habits of the old society from among the people ... At present the representatives of the bourgeoisie, the bourgeois 'scholars' and 'authorities' in China, are dreaming precisely of restoring capitalism. Though their political rule has been toppled, they're still desperately trying to maintain their academic 'authority', mould public opinion for a comeback and win over the masses, the youth and generations yet unborn from us ... In the Great Proletarian Cultural Revolution a most important task is to transform the old educational system and the old principles and methods of teaching ... The phenomenon of our schools being dominated by bourgeois intellectuals must be completely changed.

SOURCE 2

From The Private Life of Chairman Mao, the autobiography of Zhisui Li. Li was Mao's personal physician. For over twenty years, he travelled across China, accompanying Mao wherever he went, although as an educated doctor, he was in constant fear of being denounced as a class enemy. He based the book on memories of his journals written during his time with Mao, which he destroyed for fear that the Red Guards would find them.

Mao was pursuing a two-pronged attack. He was calling upon the politburo standing committee to criticize leading bourgeois intellectuals. At the same time, he was going outside the standing committee and the party hierarchy to foster a rival group centring around his closest allies – Jiang Qing and Kang Sheng in particular – whose task was to attack Mao's enemies within the standing committee and the central secretariat of the party. The move was unprecedented. Never before had Mao launched an all-out attack against such high-level officials ... The focus of the Cultural Revolution was shifting. Mao was launching what he called a 'vigorous attack' on bourgeois elements within the party, the government and the army. Liu Shaoqi, China's head of state ... had not only been purged but in October 1968 had been expelled from the party and subjected to gross abuse. In April 1969, I did not know where Liu was and would have been afraid to ask. Later, long after the party meeting was over, I learned that he had been shipped to Kaifeng, in October 1969, seriously ill, and died the following month. His illness untreated. Deng Xiaoping, too, had been purged. The politburo had been decimated.

Both sources are useful to a historian investigating the reasons why Mao launched the Cultural Revolution in 1965 because they address a range of different motives for Mao's actions. What is more, they are written from starkly different perspectives and with very different objectives. Source 1 is an official, public announcement by the Central Committee of the Communist Party at the time of time of the launching of the Cultural Revolution. In contrast, Source 2 is an extract from the memoirs of Mao's physician, based upon journal notes made from years of personal observation of Mao himself. It was published years after the Cultural Revolution. In this sense, the two documents combine to help us understand Mao's actions from different angles: both the publicly stated aims of the Cultural Revolution, namely to revise China's traditions and culture, and also the political motivations of Mao and his attempt to 'rectify' the Party. However, neither source refers specifically to fact that Mao was greatly motivated by his desire to remove his personal rivals such as Liu Shaoqi and Deng Xiaoping, who were resented. Mao was greatly motivated by his desire to reclaim power from these rivals. Therefore, there are limits as to how much a historian could uncover Mao's selfish motivations from considering the sources.

Both sources are useful in that they indicate that the Cultural Revolution was motivated by Mao's desire to create violent upheaval, which it most certainly did. In Source 2 the writer refers to Mao's desire to launch a 'two-pronged attack'. One of the targets was what Source 2 calls 'bourgeois elements', a term used to refer to anyone associated with traditional, old-fashioned ways of thinking whom Mao viewed as plotting to return China to its repressive, pre-Communist social hierarchy and economic inequality. However, the source does present difficulties for the historian. Dr Li was a physician, not a political leader, so would not necessarily possess detailed insight into Mao's precise political motivations. Furthermore, the book was based on recollections of notes recorded in a journal that was destroyed before the book was published. The book was published in the United States and has been criticised for its sensationalised approach. It refers specifically to Mao's plotting together with Jiang Qing and Kang Sheng. This plotting was aimed at targeting Mao's rivals such as Lui and Deng, whom Mao blamed for his reduced authority after the failure of the Great Leap Forward. However, this plotting was secret and therefore Dr Li cannot provide a detailed evaluation of its importance. Later, Jiang Qing accused Dr Li of attempting to poison her and tried to have him arrested. He certainly has a personal motivation to suggest that Jiang Qing was at least in part responsible for the violence of the Cultural Revolution. As an educated physician, Dr Li was at risk of being targeted by the Cultural Revolution, which might explain his focus on Mao's violent aims.

The utility of Source 1 might also be questioned. At this time the Central Committee of the Communist Party was dominated by Mao and acted as a 'rubber stamp': instead of meeting to debate policy options, by 1966 such was Mao's personal prestige and effective weakening of his opponents, the Central Committee met only to agree with whatever policies Mao had demanded. A public statement, it simply asserts the rationale Mao decided to give for the Cultural Revolution: that he wanted to 'clear away the evil habits of the old society from among the people'. This is correct: Mao did want to radically alter Chinese culture, but in reality he was creating a fear of 'evil habits' so that he could accuse his opponents of defending them and use this as an excuse to turn the Red Guards against them.

Initial contrast between nature, origin and purpose of the two sources.

Initial judgement made about the limitations of the sources for the enquiry.

Source extracts selected to support the point.

Evaluation of the 'weight' that should be attributed to the source.

Historical context used to illuminate the discussion of the sources' value.

Source 2 is useful to this enquiry because it does give a personal insight into Mao's private actions. Dr Li worked for Mao for 22 years, accompanying him on trips and diplomatic visits. He lived alongside Mao in the Zhongnanhai, the complex used previously by the Emperor of China, and met with him daily. He refers to Mao's 'unprecedented' attack against Mao's enemies 'within the standing committee and the central secretariat of the Party'. This was most certainly a key reason that Mao launched the Cultural Revolution. He feared that the Party had become overly 'bureaucratic' and was no longer sufficiently revolutionary. Mao had often referred to the need for a 'constant revolution' and purging of officials who were no longer sufficiently radical and evidence suggests that this was indeed a key motivation: 70 per cent of provincial and regional officials were purged and only nine out of 23 members of the Politburo in 1966 were not purged. Source 1 refers to 'demolishing all the old ideology and culture and all the old customs and habits'. From this we can infer that Mao wanted to destroy concepts like ancestor worship, respect for elders and religious sentiment such as Buddhism in Tibet. Mao certainly was motivated by his hatred of traditional Chinese culture: he launched the attack on the Four Olds: culture, ideas, habits and customs. Religious artefacts and temples were destroyed or defaced. Ancient literature was destroyed. Anyone who represented the old hierarchy, such as teachers or Buddhist monks in Tibet, were attacked. Anyone who might harbour traditional ideas such as Confucianism were liable to become victims of the Red Guards.

Own knowledge used to draw inferences.

Use of detailed knowledge to support source interpretation.

Finally, both sources are of limited value because neither of them deals with one of the most important reasons why Mao launched the Cultural Revolution. After the disastrous failure of the Great Leap Forward, Mao was sidelined from politics and less radical leaders like Liu Shaoqi, Deng Xiaoping and Zhou Enlai took over. Mao was jealous and feared that the achievements of the Communist revolution that he had spent so much of his life creating would be destroyed by those he damned as 'capitalist roaders'. Complaining that he was 'treated like a dead ancestor', he plotted against them, encouraging a hatred of 'old' culture and then convincing the Red Guards that his enemies at the top of the Party were sympathetic to it and had to be destroyed. He needed to create a desire to rid China of 'old habits', providing an excuse to turn the Red Guards against his opponents because Liu, Deng and Zhou were very powerful and long-term allies: he could not simply remove them without the mass mobilisation of his radical supporters to do his violent bidding. One particular reason it was launched in 1966 was that Mao was getting old: he realised that he had to act fast to protect his revolution. Source 2 does address the desire to 'rectify' the Party more than Source 1 does, but neither source sufficiently addresses this selfish, personal desire to re-establish his power which was undoubtedly a very important reason why Mao launched the Cultural Revolution in 1966.

Historical context used to discuss limitations of the source.

Use of detailed own knowledge to address weaknesses of the source.

Focus on the date: students must be aware that the answer must not only say why Mao launched the Cultural Revolution, but why he did so at that particular time.

Overall, both sources are useful as they provide evidence from differing perspectives as to why Mao launched the Cultural Revolution. However, Source 1 provides only a superficial analysis, and is essentially propaganda to hide Mao's true political motivations. It should not be dismissed, though: Mao did want to 'transform China's customs and habits' but this was not his overriding motivation. Source 2 is a viable, personal perspective, but from a doctor rather than someone closely involved in the political decision-making process. Finally, both sources are limited because they fail to sufficiently address the most important motivation for Mao's launching of the Cultural Revolution: namely his jealous desire to remove his opponents and return once against to political power.

Comparison of the utility of the two sources.

Conclusion provides an over-arching judgement of the utility of the sources, addressing both their value and also their limitations for the historian investigating Mao's motives for launching the Cultural Revolution.

This answer is awarded a mark in Level 5 as it interrogates the evidence of both sources with confidence and discrimination and deploys contextual knowledge to illuminate the value and limitations of the sources, with reference to the values and assumptions of the period. Its evaluation is based on valid criteria and the judgement takes into account different degrees of certainty.

What makes a good answer?

You have now considered two high-level essays. Use these essays to make a bullet-pointed list of the characteristics of a top-level essay. Use this list when planning and writing your own practice exam essays.

4 Social and cultural changes, 1949–76

The changing status of women

Before 1949, Chinese women had only a subservient role within society:

- The birth of a daughter was not considered a cause for celebration: many baby girls were victims of infanticide.
- Arranged marriages were common. Once married, a wife might have to share her husband with a concubine – a live-in mistress kept for sexual favours – while the wife carried out domestic chores.
- Women were subject to the three obediences: a woman was to be subservient to her father when she was young, to her husband when she was married and to her sons after she became a mother.
- Girls were not provided with educational opportunities. One survey of rural China in the 1930s suggested that only 1 per cent of females over the age of seven had acquired basic literacy skills, in comparison with 30 per cent for males.

Foot binding

Many women were physically crippled by the practice of foot binding. A girl would often have her feet bound at the age of six, her toes turned under her feet and held there by tightly wound bandages. The process was designed to stunt their growth because small feet were considered to be sexually appealing to prospective suitors, who would be willing to pay a higher 'bride-price' for a more attractive wife.

The 1950 Marriage Law

Mao attacked the 'rottenness of the marriage system' with 'no freedom of choice in love'. 'Women', Mao remarked, 'hold up half the sky'. He damned arranged marriages as 'indirect rape'. Therefore in 1950 he introduced the New Marriage Law. As a result:

- Concubinage and arranged marriages were banned.
- Husbands and wives were to have equal status in the home.
- The extraction of money or gifts in return for marriage was prohibited.
- Arranged marriages were banned.
- A wife could inherit her husband's property.
- Divorce was made much easier.

The New Marriage Law was not entirely effective, however. The law led to increased divorce rates and husbands lost what they perceived as a financial investment. Violence broke out in poorer peasant families as armed mobs attempted to violently reclaim divorced wives. Property rights gained by the law were lost when Mao collectivised private land holdings in the mid-1950s.

The impact of collectivisation and the communes on women's lives

Agricultural collectivisation took land out of private ownership and into state control. Later, people were moved into giant farming communities called communes. The property rights that were provided by the New Marriage Law became irrelevant when collectivisation and the commune system were introduced.

Women were forced to work on the land. This was meant to make them equal with men but they still took responsibility for domestic chores. They were forced to do tasks that they were physically ill-suited for, such as ploughing fields. Mothers left their children at communal kindergartens, where conditions were poor and dirty and the staff were not well trained. Diseases and deaths were commonplace.

- During the famine of the late 1950s the communes provided very little food for women. Many turned to prostitution to buy food, while others committed suicide.
- Women received little food from the communal kitchens, which was allocated based on work points, i.e. the amount of physical labour performed.
- Sexual abuse was common within the communes. Expectant mothers were forced to work throughout their pregnancy, which often resulted in miscarriages.

! Spot the mistake

Below is a sample exam-style question and a paragraph written in answer to this question. Why does this paragraph not get into Level 5? Once you have identified the mistake, rewrite the paragraph so that it displays the qualities of Level 5. The mark scheme on page 82 will help you.

'The 1950 Marriage Law ensured that women were treated as equals in China in 1949–58.' How far do you agree with this view?

To some extent, the 1950 Marriage Law ensured that women were treated as equals of men in China between 1949 and 1958. The law led to women being allowed legal rights that meant they could not be forced into relationships that they did not want and were free to make their own choices and to earn their own money. In this way, the law made them completely equal.

⦿ Spectrum of importance

Below is a sample exam question and a list of general points which could be used to answer the question. Use your own knowledge and the information on the opposite page to reach a judgement about the importance of these general points to the question posed. Write numbers on the spectrum below to indicate their relative importance. Having done this, write a brief justification of your placement, explaining why some of these factors are more important than others. The resulting diagram could form the basis of an essay plan.

How far did the lives of Chinese women improve in 1949–62?

1 Arranged marriages were banned.

2 Women were expected to do the same amount of work as men.

3 Childcare facilities and communal food halls were created during the Great Leap Forward.

4 Women were given the right to own property.

←——→

Least important   Most important

The nature and extent of change

From an early age, Mao had been critical of the subservient role that Chinese society and politics afforded to women. The CCP called women 'an indispensable force in defeating the enemy and building a new China'. Did his policies really improve the situation of Chinese women?

The Women's Association

Mao's belief in mobilisation of the masses was applied to women. The Women's Association was dedicated to encouraging political activism among women. It had an official membership of 76 million. It campaigned against prostitution and domestic violence, encouraging women to confront and denounce men who had beaten their wives.

Changes in marriage

There is some evidence to suggest that the New Marriage Law and propaganda were effective. Statistics show that by the early 1960s, child marriages and organised marriages had become very rare.

Changes in education

The Communist state also succeeded in encouraging more families to send their daughters to school. Previously there was no incentive to send them because they would soon be leaving home: they would rather that they worked in productive labour than receive an education for which the parents would experience no economic benefit. One sample of rural girls who started school between 1929 and 1949 showed that only 38 per cent completed their primary education; in contrast, 100 per cent of those starting after 1959 did so. By 1978, 45 per cent of primary school children were girls.

Military service

The Communist regime created new military academies to train a modern army. The PLA provided an opportunity for women. Young women were encouraged to join. They could escape rural poverty and possibly be promoted to officer rank, a degree of status unheard of for women in China before 1949.

Evidence of improvement in the status of women

- Many women took advantage of the opportunities provided by the new regime. They took the chance to escape unhappy marriages through divorce. No longer trapped in arranged marriages, some sought relationships for love or for personal gain. Some courted Party cadres because they knew that the relationship could improve their economic security and social opportunities.
- One example of women's greater sense of self-confidence was their willingness to stand up and declare their grievances at the 'speak bitterness' meetings organised to denounce the regime's enemies. This opportunity to publicly declare an opinion was a major change and some women found it empowering.
- Women became politicised during the Cultural Revolution: the wearing of the Maoist uniform created a sense of equality and young women could travel across China and be given important leadership roles in the Red Guards. Women like Jiang Qing could even rise to hold leadership roles in the Party.
- Maoist propaganda challenged traditional gender views. Ballets like *Red Detachment of Women* glorified women as heroes fighting in the Civil War.

The problems of changing traditional views

Traditional male attitudes were slow to change: alongside the work that the Communist regime expected women to do, husbands still saw domestic work and childcare as women's work. Many Party cadres shared the traditional views of women. They did not enforce legislation like the New Marriage Law. Communist leaders like **Ding Ling** complained that women were not treated equally even by their fellow Communists. **Song Qingling**, a prominent, high-ranking official, complained that her views were not treated equally. Traditional practices such as arranged marriages and foot binding continued in remote areas, far from Beijing, like Xingjiang.

Quick quizzes at **www.hoddereducation.co.uk/myrevisionnotes**

Spot the mistake

a

Below is a sample exam question and a paragraph written in answer to this question. Why does this paragraph not get into Level 4? Once you have identified the mistake, rewrite the paragraph so that it displays the qualities of Level 4. The mark scheme on page 82 will help you.

How far do you agree the lives of Chinese women improved in the years 1949–76?

> Women's lives in China changed a great deal between 1949 and 1976. The New Marriage Law was introduced in 1950. It was very radical, altering completely the status of women. Young women became leaders of the Red Guards during the Cultural Revolution. Women like Song Qingling and Jiang Qing became leaders in the Communist Party. Women's lives were very different from the time before Mao: they could own land and join the PLA. They could get help with childcare because they were encouraged to place their children into kindergartens set up by the Communist party in the Communes.

Eliminate irrelevance

a

Below is a sample exam-style question and a paragraph written in answer to this question. Read the paragraph and identify parts that are not directly relevant to the question. Draw a line through the information that is irrelevant and justify your deletions in the margin.

How far was gender equality achieved in China in the years 1949–76?

> Some progress had been made towards legal gender equality by 1976. The 1950 Marriage Law made men and women legally equal partners in marriage, made divorce rights legal and prevented arranged marriages. Mao had long talked about how much he wanted to create legal authority. In 1913 he had written about his dislike of arranged marriages, calling them a form of slavery. He had himself had a marriage arranged by his family, though he never considered the bride to be his true wife. However, despite the 1950 Marriage Law, in traditional rural communities this legal authority did not always mean that women were treated equally. Traditional views of women as subservient remained, despite the efforts of the Women's Association, whose representatives were sent to the countryside to educate the peasants. The least progress was made in Islamic areas like Xinjiang. Here, arranged marriages were an important custom and continued regardless of legal changes. During the Cultural Revolution, some young women became Red Guards, giving them status, authority and respect that they had not previously had.

Educational reform

The standard of education in China in 1949 was very poor. One contemporary study of education in rural China showed that:

- Only 45.2 per cent of males and only 2.2 per cent of females had received any schooling.
- Males attended on average four years of schooling. Those females who did receive schooling attended for three years.
- Eighty per cent of the population were illiterate.
- When children were educated, many received a classical education based on Confucian concepts. Practical subjects required by a modern economy such as arithmetic and science were not included.
- The system remained elitist: the best kindergartens and primary schools were located in the cities' wealthier neighbourhoods, charged prohibitive tuition fees and set entrance examinations that reduced access.

The growth of literacy

Once in power, the Communist regime sought to radically alter the situation. A national primary school system was introduced for the first time. Between 1949 and 1957, the number of primary school students increased from approximately 26 million to 64 million. The literacy rate stood at 64 per cent by 1964. Winter schools provided short courses for adult peasants. The Party claimed that 42 million peasants attended in the winter of 1951–52. There was a lack of scientists, doctors and technical experts, so universities focused on producing more of them. New polytechnics and engineering institutes were created. Many were sent to Russia to train at universities there.

Pinyin

The Chinese language was very difficult to learn. Instead of an alphabet, it used ideograms, pictures that represented words. These symbols varied greatly from region to region to the point where Chinese people from different parts of the country could not understand each other at all. A new form of written language was introduced in order to simplify the traditional and highly complex characters. Called Pinyin, it became the official language of the whole of China.

The failures of educational reform

The education system remained elitist. Key Schools were established, where students had to pass an entrance exam, that attracted the brightest pupils and best teachers. Despite promises to provide greater opportunities for all, they became the preserve of children of government officials. Education remained woefully underfunded: just 6.4 per cent of the budget was spent on culture and education in 1952. The standard of teaching in rural schools was also very poor: many teachers tasked with spreading literacy were barely educated themselves.

The winter schools were not effective in creating literacy since many peasants forgot what they had learned from one winter to the next. During the Great Leap Forward, many students could not attend school because they were working on the backyard furnaces.

The collapse of education after 1966

During the Cultural Revolution, schools and universities closed. Up to 130 million young people received no formal education. Many joined the Red Guards, travelling across the country to attend rallies or struggle meetings to denounce 'demons and monsters', terms used to describe anyone who refused to abandon the 'Four Olds'. As educated representatives of traditional authority, teachers were often victims of their revolutionary violence. Many were killed and books were destroyed. After the Red Guards were disbanded, many did not return to school. Instead they were sent to the countryside to work alongside the peasants. Again, the old elitism remained: children of Party members were able to use their connections to return to their old lives in the cities. Those who remained lived a life of rural poverty.

❶ You're the examiner

Below is a sample exam-style question and a paragraph written in answer to this question. Read the paragraph and the mark scheme provided on page 82. Decide which level you would award the paragraph. Write the level below, along with a justification for your choice.

How far did education improve in China, in the years 1949–76?

Education did not improve in China to a significant extent between 1949 and 1976. Despite promises made in the Common Programme to improve education, the government spent just 6.4 per cent of its budget on education and culture. A national primary school was introduced and Pinyin did help improve literacy rates from 20 per cent in 1949 to 64 per cent in 1964. However, the standard of teaching was still low and many peasants simply forgot what they were taught in night schools. The Key Schools were elitist, open only to Party leaders and government officials. During the Great Leap Forward, students abandoned their studies to work in the fields or on the backyard furnaces. The Cultural Revolution led to the closure of schools and the murder of many teachers. When the revolution ended, the Red Guards were sent for re-education in the countryside, to learn practical skills alongside the peasants.

Level:

Reasons for choosing this level:

_____

_____

❶ Complete the paragraph

Below is a sample exam question and a paragraph written in answer to this question. The paragraph contains a point and specific examples, but lacks a concluding analytical link back to the question. Complete the paragraph adding this link in the space provided.

To what extent did the Communist government improve the standard of education in China in the years 1949–76?

The government carried out several reforms to the system of education. Primary schools were established throughout the country, along with courses for adult education. These reforms aimed at improving national standards of literacy. The brightest children were given an advanced education by the best teachers. During the Cultural Revolution, education in China collapsed as schools and universities closed for two years. Overall, therefore ...

_____

_____

Health care

Public health provision in China was extremely rudimentary. Health care in rural China was practically non-existent: many peasants had never seen a trained doctor and preferred to rely on ancient herbal cures to heal their illnesses. With so many peasants living on the verge of starvation, their immune systems easily succumbed to epidemic disease. Waterborne diseases like typhoid, cholera and dysentery were rife. Ignorance played a part: human manure was the main source of fertiliser.

The barefoot doctors

Mao introduced the system of barefoot doctors: paramedics sent to rural areas to provide basic care to the peasants. These 'doctors' were trained intensively for just six months. They were cheap to train, focusing mainly on practical skills such as improving hygiene, stopping the spread of disease and contraception. They could provide only rudimentary health care and village clinics had little equipment and low supplies of medicine. Despite being only barely trained students, they were often the only source of medical care in the village. During Mao's rule, many Chinese people were finally treated by a trained doctor for the first time. They helped to educate peasants in modern health ideas. In total, by 1973 over a million new doctors had been trained.

Successes of health care reform

- The CCP launched Patriotic Health Movements that sent Party members into the countryside to educate peasants in how to prevent illness in the first place. Posters taught illiterate peasants how to catch rats and mosquitoes or dig deep wells to collect drinking water while pointing out the importance of personal hygiene. The use of human waste as fertiliser was discouraged.
- Villages were mobilised in collective efforts to drain swamps that bred malaria.
- Smallpox, cholera, typhus, typhoid fever, plague and leprosy were practically eliminated. Cases of tuberculosis and parasitic diseases like schistosomiasis, a deadly disease carried by snails, were reduced.
- Life expectancy rose and infant mortality fell.
- Anti-drug campaigns greatly reduced the sale and use of opium.

Failures of health care reform

- There was still very uneven health provision between rural and urban China. Western-style hospitals were centred in the cities only. Health care in rural areas or isolated peasant communities remained inadequate.
- During the Great Leap Forward, communes established medical clinics but the terrible impact of the famine negated the health benefits.
- Many doctors were attacked during the Antis campaigns of the 1950s and sent to the Laogai.
- Doctors were denounced during the Cultural Revolution. Some doctors cancelled operations, choosing to undertake manual labour like cleaning toilets in an attempt to show that they did not believe themselves to be superior to the workers.

Delete as applicable

Below is a sample exam-style question and a paragraph written in answer to this question. Read the paragraph and decide which of the possible options (in bold) is most appropriate. Delete the least appropriate options and complete the paragraph by justifying your selection.

How far did the Communist government's reforms improve the health of the Chinese people in the years 1949–76?

The Communist government's reforms had a **great/fair/limited** impact on the health of the Chinese people between these dates. The reforms did help educate the Chinese people to help prevent the spread of disease. Patriotic Health Movements taught them to prevent the spread of disease. They were taught to stop using human waste as fertiliser and to dig deep wells to collect water. Posters taught them how to catch vermin and to drain the swamps that bread the mosquitoes that spread malaria. The Women's Association played a key role in improving the standard of maternity care for women, reducing the risk of childbirth and lowering the infant mortality rate. However, what modern hospitals that there were helped only the people in the big cities. Rural peasant communities had only basic clinics. Many peasants still relied on traditional Chinese herbal medicine. The government only spent a tiny amount of money on health care, so the policies had to focus mainly on prevention rather than actual treatment. Clearly, the government reforms had a **great/fair/limited** impact on the health of the Chinese people since

_____

_____

Developing an argument

Below is a sample exam-style question, a list of key points to be made in the essay, and a simple introduction and conclusion for the essay. Read the question, the key points and the introduction and conclusion. Rewrite the introduction and the conclusion in order to develop an argument.

How successful were the changes in health care provision in the years 1949–76?

Key points
- Success: improved understanding of importance of personal hygiene.
- Weakness: lack of access to modern medicine for rural communities.
- Success: improved standard of midwifery.
- Weakness: lack of funding meant a shortage of medicines.
- Success: barefoot doctors scheme provided over a million new doctors to rural areas.
- Weakness: barefoot doctors received only six months' basic training.

Introduction:

The Communist government's health care reforms saw successes and failures in the period 1949–76. The successes were the Patriotic Health Movements that improved the health care literacy of the Chinese people, improvements in midwife care and the barefoot doctors scheme. The weaknesses of the reforms were the fact that lack of funding meant that there was a lack of medicine, rural care was very basic and although the barefoot doctors did provide some care, they were poorly trained and equipped.

Conclusion:

The Chinese government's health care reforms saw successes and failures in the period 1949–76. Overall, the campaign was successful.

Cultural change 1

Mao intended to create a form of culture which would appeal to the mass of Chinese workers and peasants, not simply the educated elite. He insisted that those who contributed to traditional Chinese cultural activities, such as art and music, would be pressed into the service of a culture which was accessible to all. In this, as in many other ways, Mao was following the example of Stalin in the USSR. In the 1930s, Stalin had developed cultural forms, known collectively as Socialist Realism, which glorified Communist achievements. Mao wanted to follow a similar path, with culture serving a political rather than an artistic purpose.

Attacks on traditional culture in towns and countryside

Mao believed that culture could be used as a way of controlling the thoughts of the people and to inculcate Communist ideology. Many features of traditional culture were simply swept away. The land reforms of the 1950s and the destruction of village life brought an end to traditional festivals such as the Lantern Festival, the New Year and the celebration of the seasons. The reunification campaigns had a devastating effect on the ancient cultures of both Tibet and Xinjiang, respectively based on Lamaism and Islam. Both Confucianism and ancestor worship were condemned as backward superstitions. **Agit-prop** groups toured the country trying to convince people to abandon their old traditions, customs and habits and instead follow Communism. The ability of the Communist Party to monitor and control culture was greatly enhanced when the peasants were forced into communes during the Great Leap Forward.

In August 1966, Mao launched the 'Four Olds' campaign to destroy so-called old ideas, old culture, old customs and old habits. Religious artefacts and temples were destroyed, philosophical books were burnt. Religious shrines in peasant houses were replaced by pictures of Mao. Street names that derived from folk traditions, such as 'Fortune and Longevity Road' were renamed. Customs such as paying respects by burning paper money or incense at the graves of ancestors during the Qingming festival were discouraged. Despite the ferocity of the Four Olds campaign, the Communists were not entirely successful, because customs and traditions were too engrained.

The role of Jiang Qing

In 1966, Mao appointed Jiang Qing, his fourth wife, to the CCRG. Her ambition was to destroy traditional Chinese culture and replace it with revolutionary Communism.

She imposed censorship of music, theatre and art, banning any performances that encouraged old-fashioned 'feudal' ideas such as romance, aspirations for wealth and property or respect for family. Her previous career as an actress meant that she believed that she was qualified to rewrite performances: she sometimes attended rehearsals and gave orders on how the actors could portray Communism more positively. Plays were rewritten to include characters who supported Communist ideas. Before the Cultural Revolution, Jiang Qing did not have a significant political role. Her new role as 'Cultural Tsar' gave her huge power and influence and led to her becoming one of the most important leaders in China. In 1969, she joined the Politburo and later became a member of the infamous Gang of Four, the radicals who hoped to take over China after Mao. She used the Cultural Revolution as a cover to purge anyone who knew about her bourgeois past as an actress in Shanghai. She attacked them so they would not be able to ruin her attempt to increase her own power. She had power only because of her relationship with Mao. But since Mao was elderly, she needed to develop her own political authority if she was to survive after his death. She used the Cultural Revolution both as an attempt to intimidate her enemies and to rid herself of anyone who might prevent her rise to power. However, Jiang Qing was also guilty of using violence for her own ends.

What were Madame Mao's motives?

Jiang Qing became a figure of hate because of the violent fervour with which she attacked her opponents. However, she later claimed to be acting on direct orders from Mao: 'I was Chairman Mao's dog', she claimed. 'Whomever Chairman Mao asked me to bite, I bit.' She certainly was acting according to Mao's wishes but it was also true that the fervour with which she attacked 'bourgeois' culture was motivated by a personal vendetta: for example, she attacked rivals from her acting past and associates who knew about her embarrassing bourgeois past, including rumours that she had slept with directors to win parts when she was an actress in Shanghai in the 1920s.

! Delete as applicable   a

Below is a sample exam-style question and a paragraph written in answer to this question. Read the paragraph and decide which of the possible options (in bold) is most appropriate. Delete the least appropriate options and complete the paragraph by justifying your selection.

· How far do you agree that Jiang Qing succeeded in replacing old art and culture with one based on Communism?

Jiang Qing did replace old Chinese art and culture with one based on Communism to a **significant/partial/limited** extent. She attacked traditional theatre and opera as 'bourgeois' and 'revisionist'. Performances that included 'old-fashioned' ideas such as romance, religion or ancestor worship were banned or rewritten. Directors, composers and writers who defended traditional performances, literature and art were blacklisted or imprisoned. Some were attacked by the Red Guards and others committed suicide to escape the threats and violence. Temples and religious monuments were destroyed, as were foreign books, and all foreign plays were banned. However, many peasants were unaffected. Furthermore, old ideas such as ancestor worship were not destroyed: when Zhou Enlai died there was a spontaneous outpouring of grief during the Qingming festival, the traditional time to honour respected ancestors. Therefore, it would be accurate to say that Jiang Qing succeeded only to a **significant/partial/limited** extent in the sense that

_____

_____

i Develop the detail

Below is a sample exam-style question and paragraph written in answer to this question. The paragraph contains a limited amount of detail. Annotate the paragraph to add additional detail to the answer.

How far do you agree that the Communists failed in their attempts to destroy traditional art and culture?

The Communists' attempt to destroy traditional art and culture were a failure to some extent. Jiang Qing used censorship for this purpose and encouraged plays and operas that had a Communist message. Plays glorified Communism, such as plays that featured Communist heroes fighting the Japanese. The Red Guards were also used to attack cultural sites like temples or religious monuments. While art and culture were replaced and destroyed, the Communists were not completely successful. Despite the campaigns, many Chinese people kept believing their old ideas.

Cultural change 2

The imposition of revolutionary art and culture

Performances of foreign works were banned. Directors, writers and directors were fired or blacklisted. Some were attacked by the Red Guards and others committed suicide to escape the violence. All new plays and operas glorified Communism. Works that featured traditional habits, customs and ideas were replaced by plays and operas that advocated Communist ideology. 'Make it revolutionary or ban it' was the slogan. Eight new 'model dramas' were created. The new 'revolutionary shows' featured Communist characters: *Taking Tiger Mountain by Strategy* featured an undercover Communist soldier infiltrating and defeating bandits, while *The Legend of the Red Lantern* told the story of Communist agents resisting a Japanese invasion. Old traditions and beliefs were derided as superstitions: for example, in *Romance on the Milky Way*, a groom, referring to the belief that prospects for a good marriage would be helped by scheduling the wedding for a 'lucky' day, declares 'We must pick an auspicious day', for which his future sister-in-law, a good Communist, scolds him for being 'superstitious'.

Some of the ballets were turned into movies. In *Red Detachment of Women*, the heroine, a poor peasant, escapes from an evil landlord who had imprisoned her for failing to pay her exorbitant rent. She becomes the leader of a women's Red Army detachment, helped by a dashing Party cadre. *The East is Red*, a sweeping dance epic, took Mao's cult of personality to bizarre levels. Tracing the rise of the Communist Party from obscurity to victory in the Civil War, the title song announced Mao to be 'The People's Saviour' and claimed that 'Without the Communist Party, there would be no China.' Propaganda teams travelled to villages with new models of portable projectors to show the films. Evidence suggests that in Guangdong province in 1966, villagers watched four films. By 1974, they watched ten per year. The film version of *Taking Tiger Mountain* had been seen by 7.3 billion people – or seven times by each Chinese person!

There were only eight new operas and plays allowed. China during the Cultural Revolution has been described as a 'cultural desert' that, one biographer of Jiang Qing wrote, 'turned the minds of the audience to "mashed potatoes"'. After the initial interest, the lack of diversity became boring: it led to 'eight hundred million people watching eight shows' as one joke put it. Even Communist leaders grumbled: Deng Xiaoping complained that 'people want to go to the theatre to relax' but instead 'you find yourself in a battlefield'. Part of the reason for the incredibly high audience figures was that aside from Maoist propaganda films, there was nothing else to watch! However, the new culture did not reach all Chinese people: the government feared that too much disruption would reduce agricultural production and so many peasants were not greatly involved. It has been noted that when the PLA went to the countryside to help the peasants, many had never even heard of the Cultural Revolution.

Conclusion

Mao's rule proved to be disastrous for Chinese culture. He believed that culture was a tool by which societies could be controlled or remade. Therefore, all culture had to proclaim the greatness of the Communist Party and enforce ideological commitment to its policies. Mao had no respect for the traditions of Chinese life, which were brutally swept aside and replaced with a Communist culture which extolled the successes of Communist rule, the heroism of the PLA and the role of ordinary people within national life. Pre-revolutionary books were banned, and music and popular songs praised both Mao and the CCP. The culture of traditional village life was targeted. Old customs and beliefs such as Confucianism or respect for family elders were damned as superstitions. This control was heightened during the push for collectivisation, as traditional ways of life were radically altered. During the Cultural Revolution, Jiang Qing had succeeded in her aim of creating a new Communist culture, but the old traditions proved hard to suppress, and in the years since Mao's death many of these old customs have been revived, often with a renewed vigour.

! Identify the concept   a

Below are five sample exam questions based on some of the following concepts:

- Cause – questions concern the reasons for something, or why something happened.
- Consequence – questions concern the impact of an event, an action or a policy.
- Change/continuity – questions ask you to investigate the extent to which things changed or stayed the same.
- Similarity/difference – questions ask you to investigate the extent to which two events, actions or policies were similar.
- Significance – questions concern the importance of an event, an action or a policy.

Read each of the questions and work out which of the concepts they are based on.

'Communist policies had little impact on Chinese culture in the period 1965–76.' How far do you agree with this statement?

How far did Communist policies towards culture change in the period 1949–76?

How accurate is it to say that the growth in influence of Jiang Qing was the most important consequence of Communist policies towards culture, 1965–76?

To what extent was Mao's decision to launch the Cultural Revolution caused by his desire to remould Chinese culture?

How far do you agree that the reasons for the launching of the Hundred Flowers campaign and the Cultural Revolution were the same?

i Turning assertion into argument

Below is a sample exam question and a series of assertions. Read the exam question and then add a justification to each of the assertions to turn it into an argument.

How far did the Communist Party successfully remould Chinese culture between 1949 and 76?

There were dramatic changes in Chinese culture during the Great Leap Forward because

_____

_____

The land reform programme led to a significant change in traditional peasant culture because

_____

_____

Jiang Qing successfully remade culture but her 'model plays' did not win many supporters for Communism because

_____

_____

The outpouring of grief that marked the death of Zhou Enlai was clear evidence that the Communist Party had failed to eradicate old beliefs and customs.

_____

Attacks on Buddhism, Confucianism and ancestor worship

The Communist Party viewed religious belief as a form of feudal superstition, representing the old and outdated views that Communism wanted to sweep away. In Marxist theory religion was derided as an 'opiate', a drug used by the bourgeois elite to pacify the workers and peasants and prevent them from revolting. Furthermore, Christianity was resented as a Western imposition, used by the capitalist West to 'brainwash' the Chinese into subservience. The influence of the mullahs in Xinjiang and Buddhist priests in Tibet was viewed as a political challenge to the Communist government's desire to create the 'New China'. Attacks on all forms of religious belief and practices began as soon as the CCP came to power.

Buddhism

Buddhism had played an important contributing role in the development of culture and society for over a thousand years. Most Buddhists were in Tibet where the form of Buddhism, called Lamaism, underpinned Tibetans' sense of independence and national identity. The Communist government could not allow this. When the PLA launched the reunification campaigns of the 1950s, Buddhist monasteries in Tibet were attacked and monks sent to the Laogai to be 'reformed'. The reason was not entirely related to religion: Tibet borders India, an ally of the West and a country with which China had previously had a number of border disputes. Temples were taken over and converted for other uses; during the Great Leap Forward land was confiscated and given to the communes, and monks were forced to take up hard physical labour. Many starved or were forced to abandon their principles and join the PLA. By the end of the Cultural Revolution, few temples or shrines remained. Once again, the regime was not entirely successful in changing the long-held beliefs of the people.

Confucianism

Confucius was a Chinese philosopher in the fifth century BC. Confucianism is a philosophical outlook on life rather than a set of religious beliefs. Confucius promoted family and kinship values, respect for others and the importance of ancestor worship. His ideas received widespread acceptance and shaped the thinking and behaviour of millions of Chinese for 2,500 years. Confucianism was condemned by the CCP long before 1949, and came under constant attack by Mao and his government. Annual ceremonies which commemorated Confucius were banned. During the Cultural Revolution, Red Guards destroyed many memorials to Confucius in his home town of Qufu. The anti-Confucius campaign made Confucianism a symbol for any idea that seemed backward and reactionary. Opponents that the regime wanted to denounce were publicly compared to Confucius. At the end of the Cultural Revolution, the Gang of Four used anti-Confucius propaganda to attack their opponents. Comparing a political enemy to Confucius was to suggest that they were backward in their thinking and not committed to Communist ideology. In 1973, they launched a campaign that compared Confucius with Lin Biao, the disgraced former head of the PLA. Since Lin was long dead, the campaign's target was evidently enemies like Zhou Enlai. After the turmoil of the Cultural Revolution, most people were sick of political campaigns and it was not a success.

Despite the enthusiastic attacks on Confucius and his thought from the Red Guards and from Mao himself, Confucian thought never disappeared from Chinese life and it is followed by many Chinese people today.

The New Year festival and ancestor worship

Adherence to traditions such as the celebration of New Year and the worship of ancestors was condemned by the Communists: they represented the 'old China' that was to be replaced through Communist revolution. The Communists wanted to reduce the strength of family ties: these were also an important part of Confucian thought and therefore considered backward and superstitious. Loyalty to the Party was what mattered.

The Communists attempted to dissuade people from returning to the graves of their ancestors to honour them during the Qingming festival. The tradition of giving children *hongbao* (red envelopes of money) was viewed as bourgeois. Workers were discouraged from carrying joss sticks and paper money back to their home villages. The Qingming festival was replaced by a new Communist festival, National Memorial Day. Instead of paying respect to their elders, the people were urged to honour the fallen Communist heroes who had died in the Civil War. The Communists were never entirely successful in their efforts to reduce ancestor worship. This was evident from the spontaneous outpouring of public respect for Zhou Enlai when he died. The tributes paid to Zhou in Tiananmen Square were very much like ancestor worship.

Support or challenge?

Below is a sample exam question which asks how far you agree with a specific statement. Below this is a series of general statements which are relevant to the question. Using your own knowledge and the information on the opposite page, decide whether these statements support or challenge the statement in the question and tick the appropriate box.

> How successful were the government's attempts to suppress religion and religious beliefs in the years 1949–76?

Statement	Support	Challenge
The Dalai Lama was forced to flee to India.		
Religious schools in Xinjiang were closed and replaced by government schools.		
Foreign Christian missionaries were forced to leave China.		
Patriotic Church services were poorly attended.		
Christian priests secretly performed services in private homes.		
National Memorial Day was created.		
Propaganda damned ancestor worship as 'superstition'.		
Zhou Enlai was honoured in traditional fashion during the 1976 Qingming festival.		

Explain the difference **a**

The following sources give different accounts of the government's attitudes toward religion and religious beliefs. List the ways in which the sources differ. Explain the differences between the sources using the provenance of the sources and the historical context. The provenance appears at the top of each source. Make sure you stay focused on the differences that are relevant to the question.

> How far could the historian make use of Sources 1 and 2 together to investigate the government's attitudes toward religion and religious beliefs?

Explain your answer, using both sources, the information given about them and your own knowledge of the historical context.

SOURCE 1

Extract from the 1954 Constitution of the People's Republic of China.

Article 85: All citizens of the People's Republic of China are equal before the law.

Article 87: Citizens of the PRC enjoy freedom of assembly, freedom of association, freedom of procession and freedom of demonstration.

Article 88: Citizens of the People's Republic of China enjoy freedom of religious belief.

SOURCE 2

A letter from a Catholic girl in Shanghai, written in 1956. From Richard C. Bush, Religion in Communist China *(1970).*

We, the Catholic youth, were especially sought out. We were locked up in a branch of the police bureau for interrogation and to make a confession. We were forbidden to return to our homes. We spent a week in prison, and it was very hard. After that we had to participate in the indoctrination meetings of the district. This indoctrination went on for three months. The moral hardships we underwent are indescribable. Sometimes the meetings lasted until early morning. Finally, we had to make out a written confession. That was the last thing we had to do, but it was terrifying. Now our church is entirely directed by the government. The annoyances we have to go through are innumerable, especially when we encounter the Commissar of the People whom we have to obey under pain of being declared anti-revolutionary and sent to prison.

Religion 2

Christianity

The Protestant and Catholic Churches were targeted because the Communists believed that Christianity was representative of Western imperialist ideas. The Communists created so-called 'Patriotic Church' movements. According to the propaganda, these new movements were created to organise religion for the benefit of the Chinese people. In reality, they were a way of imposing control over the Churches, and were totally controlled by the Communist government. They hung portraits of Mao in their churches. Schools and hospitals set up and run by the Churches were taken over by the government. Missionaries were forced out of the country or imprisoned. However, congregations at the Patriotic Churches were low and many clergy still organised secret Christian services, often in the homes of the congregations.

Anti-Christian repression sparked a major confrontation with the Roman Catholic Church. Communist propaganda damned the Catholic Church. It was claimed that Catholic hospitals were using patients as 'human guinea pigs' to tests out new medicines, Catholic schools were attacked for supposedly helping the United States during the Korean War and Catholic children's homes were accused of starving and torturing children. The Vatican protested the repression of Catholics and refused to accept the 'Patriotic Churches' as genuinely Catholic. The Pope threatened to excommunicate any clergy who co-operated with the Communist regime. In January 1951, there were 3,222 Catholic missionaries in China; by 1953 there were just 364. This did not mean that Christianity was destroyed, however: clergy continued to meet, in secret, in family homes.

Islam

Muslims were also targeted. Most lived in the north-western provinces of Xinjiang, Gansu and Qinghai. Islam represented a rival belief system to Communist ideology and the Communists resented the power of the mullahs, religious leaders who had great influence in their societies. They were clearly a barrier to the imposition of Communism. Predominantly Muslim Xinjiang province was an immediate target for the Communists. The PLA invaded Xinjiang in October 1949 as part of the so-called reunification campaigns. Mosque schools were closed down and government schools teaching Marxism, not the Qur'an, were set up. With the closing of these schools, the traditional Muslim teaching of theology, ritual, poetry and ethics was ended. Land was taken from mosques and redistributed. Those who resisted were imprisoned in the Laogai. The government encouraged the inward migration of Han Chinese to dilute the ethnic homogeneity of Muslim communities, especially in Xinjiang. The PLA helped to build roads into Xinjiang to help speed this ethnic dilution. The Chinese government feared that other Islamic countries like Afghanistan and Pakistan might encourage demands for independence from the PRC. During the Cultural Revolution, mosques were shut down and turned into barracks and stables. Religious leaders were tortured or given humiliating jobs like cleaning sewers. The Muslim provinces were particularly targeted because they bordered the Islamic republics of the Soviet Union and Beijing was worried that the Soviets, keen to get hold of their rich reserves of oil and gas, would encourage separatist movements to demand union with them instead. Islamic communities resisted the imposition of Communist control, in some cases through military force, and the government was forced to be more respectful of Islamic culture.

Conclusion

Religious belief was targeted from the very first days of the PRC. Damned as mere 'superstition' by the Communist government, it represented exactly the kind of 'old thinking' that they believed had held China back. The pacifistic elements of religion did not fit with the regime's focus on building Chinese military strength, while Christian beliefs meant loyalty to an alternative leader rather than Mao. The work of Christian missionaries in China represented the interference of the West. Traditional beliefs advocated subservience to family, ancestors, elders or clergy, a clear contradiction to Mao's beliefs. However, the issue was far more than spiritual. The Islamic provinces had clear strategic and economic importance, India was a Western ally, while the Papacy was an influential international foe. During the Cultural Revolution, religion was targeted as one of the 'Four Olds' and believers were liable to be imprisoned. For all their efforts, the Communists never completely eradicated religious beliefs: old attitudes and traditions were simply too engrained into Chinese culture.

● Explain the difference

The following sources give different accounts attitude to religious beliefs in China under Mao. List the ways in which the sources differ. Explain the differences between the sources using their provenance and the historical context. The provenance appears at the top of each source. Make sure you stay focused on the differences that are relevant to the question.

How far could the historian make use of Sources 1 and 2 together to investigate Communist attitudes to religious belief during Mao's rule?

Explain your answer, using both sources, the information given about them and your own knowledge of the historical context.

SOURCE 1

Li Zhisui, The Private Life of Chairman Mao (1996). Li, Mao's private doctor, spent a lot of time with Mao. Here he recalls accompanying Mao on a visit to his ancestral home during the Great Leap Forward.

I met Mao at his guest house, and we began walking down the back of the hill. Partway down, in the middle of a small pine grove, Mao stopped before a burial mound. It was only when he bowed from the waist in the traditional manner of respect that I realised we were standing before his parents' grave. Shen Tong, one of the security officers accompanying us, quickly gathered a bunch of wildflowers. Mao placed the flowers on the grave and bowed three times again. The rest of his entourage, standing behind him, bowed too. 'There used to be a tombstone here', Mao said. 'It has disappeared after all these years.' We continued walking down the hill in the direction of the Mao clan ancestral hall. Again Mao stopped, puzzled, looking for something. We were standing on the spot where the Buddhist shrine Mao had referred to so often·in our conversations once stood – the shrine his mother used to visit when he was sick, where she burned incense and fed the ashes to her son, certain of their curative powers. The tiny shrine, like the tombstone, had disappeared, torn down only months before with the establishment of the commune. The bricks were needed to build the backyard steel furnaces, and the wood had been used for fuel. Mao had fallen silent on our walk. The destruction of the shrine had saddened him. 'It's such a pity', he said. 'It should have been left alone. Without money to see doctors, poor farmers could still come and pray to the gods and eat the incense ashes. The shrine could lift their spirits, give them hope. People need this kind of help and encouragement.' I smiled when he said this, but Mao was serious. 'Don't look down on incense ashes', he said ... 'Incense ashes give people the courage to fight disease, don't you think?' People could not live without spiritual support, Mao believed.

SOURCE 2

Quentin K. Y. Huang, Now I Can Tell (1954). Huang was a Catholic bishop in China. He was arrested and imprisoned.

I was pushed and literally 'packed' into the wooden cage. It consisted of wooden bars from four to five inches in diameter, each about two inches apart. The door was closed, locked, and chained. The cage was about six by eight feet in dimension, situated in a dark, damp end of a long room. The other end of the room was used as quarters for the guards who watched us inside the cage and also those outside who were waiting for the judgement of the Commissioner of Police. Outside the wooden cage a pile of ropes, chains, and handcuffs was stored and ever ready for use on prisoners. In this small cage I found (as I later counted) 18 new companions – criminals of all classes, including thieves, robbers, murderers, counterfeiters, adulterers and, of course, the so-called 'political criminals' including myself. We were packed in like sardines, with no space for lying down or sitting; consequently, we all had to stand. When arrested, no one was able usually even to say goodbye to loved ones or to bring any necessary things except what he wore. The Communist regime provided neither water nor food for the prisoners. Conditions were the same in regards to our daily trip to the latrine ... Neglect and delay, particularly with diarrhoea cases, soon turned a part of the wooden cage into a natural latrine, filthy and foul smelling with lice, fleas, and hungry rats.

Exam focus

Below is a sample exam answer to the following A-level question. Read the answer and the comments around it. Bear these in mind when tackling the activity at the end.

How far do you agree that the policies of the CCP brought widespread benefits to Chinese society in the years 1949-58?

In the years 1949-58, Mao introduced a wide range of policies to improve Chinese society. These included gender equality as well as change to the lives of the middle classes, workers and peasants. There were certainly some benefits at the start of the period, but they could not be deemed as 'widespread'. Lack of investment and the disastrous Great Leap Forward outweighed the improvements. By the end of the period the situation of some of the groups was arguably worse than it had been at the start.

Women had little social status in 1949. They could not own property or divorce, and many were deformed by foot-binding. Few girls were allowed to go to school, and many were forced into arranged marriages or became concubines. In 1949, the CCP banned arranged marriages, concubines and foot-binding. The 1950 Marriage Law gave women the right to own property and to divorce. However, these benefits were short-lived. The New Marriage Law was not always adhered to: conservative Party cadres refused to enforce it, particularly in traditional rural communities. In Islamic Xinjiang, the practice of arranged marriages continued unaltered. Women might have become politicised, but that did not mean that they were equal: Communist leaders like Song Qing Ling and Ding Ling held important roles in the Party, but complained that their male counterparts still did not take them seriously. The right to own land was quickly removed by land reform and women's lives became even worse during the Great Leap Forward. Gender equality meant equal work, but male expectations of women's roles remained unaltered and husbands still expected women to take responsibility for the bulk of domestic work and childcare. Overall, there was little real change in the status of women in these years.

The Communists promised to improve the lives of the urban workers. The standard of housing was poor, wages were low and there was little job security. After 1952, the Five-Year Plan improved employment prospects and helped wages to rise, and food supplies to the cities were increased. These benefits came at the cost of personal freedoms, however. All workers were organised into Danwei, or work units. They organised the distribution of permits for travel and marriage as well as access to food and housing. The focus on heavy industry meant that, although they had more substantial wages, there was still a shortage of consumer goods in the shops and the famine of the late 1950s led to reduced food supplies. Most workers had previously been peasants and had travelled to the cities for work: they could not leave the cities to return to their villages and many lost their families to the famine.

For the peasants, the group whom the CCP had championed in the revolution, Mao's rule was one of false hope. There were improvements in health care: although there were still not enough doctors, rural clinics meant that many peasants were able to see a doctor for the first time in their lives. Patriotic Health Movements taught peasants how to be more hygienic, for example by digging latrines well away from housing and ending the use of human excrement as fertiliser. In 1950, the Agrarian Reform Law began the process of land redistribution. Peasants seized their landlords' farms and claimed them as their own. From 1950 to 1953, peasants were organised into Mutual Aid Teams, where around 30 families came together to pool their resources and farm the land together. This did improve the life of peasants because they were able to increase food production. In 1953, Mutual Aid Teams were combined to create Agricultural Production Co-operatives (APCs), but these benefits broke down. Peasants were now organised into groups with total strangers, which reduced their incentive

Margin comments

A focused introduction that identifies the significance of the dates and presents a judgement that shows awareness of the term 'widespread'.

Answer sets out the problems for women at the start of the essay's date range, helping the candidate to make a judgement of 'improvement'.

Addresses limitations of policies showing an awareness of the duration of the policies' effectiveness.

Paragraph ends with a judgement of how far the policies had succeeded.

Strong supporting detail including specific examples of both benefits and negatives for urban workers.

Impact of policies on middle classes in rural and urban areas addressed.

to work well, and in the years before the Great Leap Forward the APCs would only get larger. This affected production and reversed the improvements of early land reform. In 1958, all land was collectivised and peasants were forced into communes. Lack of investment in health care – it was just 1.3 per cent of state investment in 1952 – meant a shortage of medicines for the communes, and malnourishment meant that life expectancy and fertility dropped. Peasants were also used as labourers, set to work on large irrigation projects and building industrial plants. The backyard furnaces campaign meant that crops often lay in the fields, uncollected. Because of the Anti-Rightist campaign, there were no scientists or intellectuals who would dare to offer alternative policies or to set out the economic failings of Mao's policies. Because of the ideologically driven nature of Mao's policies, millions were to die during the famine.

The middle classes definitely did not benefit from Mao's policies. In rural areas, landlords were purged during the land reform programme. Millions died and their land was confiscated. These landlords were often the peasants with the most energy, commitment and education, who could have modernised Chinese agriculture by using new techniques or machines. With the introduction of the communes during the Great Leap Forward, these benefits were ignored and they were forced into harsh manual labour. In the cities, intellectuals were negatively affected by Mao's policies. In 1949, many scholars wanted to help Mao rebuild China. However, Mao disliked intellectuals since most had attended the Western-funded and -run universities pre-1949 and were usually from the traditional ruling classes. After they had helped China rebuild after decades of war, many civil servants were purged and replaced by Party cadres. An example of Mao's violently oppressive attitude to the intellectuals is the consequence of the Hundred Flowers campaign of 1956–57. Mao encouraged the intellectuals to offer their advice and comments about the progress of the revolution. When the intellectuals were critical of both the Communist Party and even Mao himself, he branded them as 'rightists' and 500,000 were sent to Laogai, a network of brutal prison camps. Attacks on intellectuals and the old ruling class showed that the CCP's policies did not benefit all of Chinese society.

In conclusion, the benefits of the Mao's policies were only short-lived and were not widespread. Although there was some improvement in the legal status of women from 1950, and the standard of living did rise for urban workers, the violent attacks on intellectuals and the middle classes, and the starvation of the peasants in order to satisfy Mao's desire for China to become a great military force, led to overall few benefits for the Chinese people. All these benefits were wiped away by the Great Leap Forward, which caused famine and destitution. This would not change until 1961, when the pragmatist President Liu Shaoqi and Deng Xiaoping would take the reins of the CCP and sacrifice ideological purity for functional policies to recover and improve China's economy.

Detailed supporting evidence referring to specific campaigns and statistics to support their impact.

Judgement addresses change over time and utilises key term from question.

Specific detail on Mao's policies towards the middle class and intellectuals.

Conclusion addresses duration of impact and widespread nature of policies, and ends with the impact of the Great Leap Forward, ensuring the answer addresses the final date in the question's date range.

This response has a strong focus on the question, detailed supporting evidence and a clear judgement that differentiates between a range of social groups and across time. It addresses the importance of the term 'widespread' in the question to present a nuanced judgement.

Reverse engineering

The best essays are based on careful plans. Read the essay and the comments and try to work out the general points of the plan used to write the essay. Once you have done this, note down the specific examples used to support each general point.

AS-level questions

How far did the lives of women improve in China during the period 1949–76?

Communist educational reforms were a complete failure in the period 1949–76.' How far do you agree?

How far did traditional attitudes and beliefs in China change in the period 1965–76?

Glossary

Agit-prop   So-called 'agitation propaganda' groups toured the countryside putting on shows, films and handing out leaflets that spread Communist political ideas.

Barefoot doctors   Doctors who received basic first-aid training and were sent out to remote rural areas where there were no trained doctors in order to provide health care to the peasants.

Big Character Poster   Handwritten posters mounted on walls used to spread propaganda.

Bourgeoisie   In Marxist thought, the bourgeoisie is a wealthy class of property owners who are dedicated to retaining their economic power and influence.

Bourgeois feudal classes   Feudal society had a power structure whereby lords demanded services or taxes from the peasants. The Communists used the term to describe an unequal society, damning anyone who defended such an unfair system as 'counter-revolutionaries'.

Capitalist roaders   A label used to refer to enemies who did not support Communism but instead wanted to take the 'capitalist road' to develop China.

Centrally planned economy   An economy where the government makes decisions such as what and how much to produce, rather than letting consumers and businesses decide.

Central Cultural Revolution Group (CCRG)   An organisation created in 1966 that was filled with Mao's supporters who wanted to take a radical path towards creating Communism. During the Cultural Revolution, it became more important than the Politburo as the main decision-making organisation of government.

Chinese Communist Party (CCP)   Founded in 1921, the CCP seized power through victory in the Civil War. In 1949, it announced the formation of the PRC. This is the ruling party in China to the present day.

Chinese People's Political Consultative Conference (CPPCC)   A conference of delegates from a range of parties, the CPPCC was called by the victorious Communists in 1949 to discuss how to organise the government of the PRC.

Cold War   A period of tension between the Western democracies and the Communist countries in the East. Instead of direct armed conflict, which was impossible because it risked a nuclear apocalypse, the two sides competed in different ways such as through propaganda, an arms race or the space race.

Collectivise   The process by which private land was taken away from its owners and controlled instead by the state.

Common Programme   Interim constitution created in 1949 which set out the structure of the new government. Replaced by a permanent written constitution in 1954.

Communists   Believers in the ideas of Karl Marx, who encouraged the working classes to revolt against capitalist employers who, he believed, repressed them. Once the upper classes had been destroyed, the workers would organise a communist state where resources were shared out.

Confucian tradition   Traditions based upon the beliefs of the philosopher Confucius, who was born in 551 BC. His ideas about ethics, family loyalty and respect for government were hugely influential in China.

Conscripted   Forced to join the armed forces. The Communist Party introduced conscription into the PLA in 1953.

Cult of personality   An idealised propaganda image created to convince the masses that a leader has near super and divine powers.

Danwei   A 'work unit' to which all Chinese workers belonged. Created by the Communists as a way to organise the workers, it controlled access to rations, housing and permits to travel or to get married.

Democratic centralism   System of government created by Russian Bolshevik leader Lenin, a synthesis of democracy and central government authority where elections for representative bodies such as local people's congresses were meant to provide an opportunity for democratic debate and discussion. However, once a decision was made by the central government, all party members had to adhere to it.

February Adverse Current   During the Cultural Revolution, radical Red Guard violence got out of hand. The 'Adverse Current' was an attempt by more conservative forces to keep the Red Guards from creating anarchy and civil war.

Gang of Four   A group of Communist leaders, including Mao's wife, Jiang Qing, who wanted to follow a radical and violent revolutionary path towards turning China into a communist country.

Grain embargo   A ban on trading grain, imposed by the United States after Chinese intervention in the Korean War.

Grain requisitioning   The process of taking food from the peasants in order to fund industrial production. The food was taken by the Party cadres: much was sold to the Soviet Union to fund the buying of modern industrial equipment. During the Great Leap Forward, levels of requisitioning became so harsh that a massive famine was created.

Great Famine   A period in 1959–61 when Mao's policies, like the Great Leap Forward, led to widespread starvation.

Hyperinflation   Out-of-control inflation whereby the value of the currency falls at such a spectacular rate as to render it practically worthless.

Kuomintang (GMD)   The official name of the Chinese Nationalist Party, which fought against Mao's Communist Party during the Civil War.

Legislature   Institution of government responsible for making laws.

Little Red Book   Collection of Mao's sayings that was published by Lin Biao. People were forced to read and recite the sayings as a way to indoctrinate them into supporting Mao.

Mao Zedong Thought   Mao's key ideas such as the belief in continuous revolution and mass mobilisation.

Mandarin   A government official in the civil service during Chinese Imperial times.

May Seventh Cadres Schools   Forced labour camps created during the Cultural Revolution.

Nationalists   The enemies of the Communists, who fought against Mao in the Chinese Civil War.

Obstructionist bureaucracy   Attempts by bureaucrats (managers) who had a vested interest in retaining their power and influence, to block or slow down revolutionary reforms.

Politburo   A senior committee in the Communist Party that had wide-ranging powers to make policy.

People's Liberation Army (PLA)   The armed forces of the PRC.

Proletarian party   A political party dedicated to defending the rights of the working class.

Right-wingers   Believers in right-wing ideas opposed to Mao, whose ideas were very radical, Communist and therefore 'left-wing'.

Secret Speech   Speech made by Soviet Leader Nikita Khrushchev in 1956. He denounced Stalin's use of terror and the creation of a cult of personality.

Sino–Soviet   Referring to relations between China and the USSR, the two largest Communist nations in the world during the twentieth century.

Soviet Union (USSR)   The Union of Soviet Socialist Republics, a Communist state created in Russia in 1922.

Space race   Competition between the capitalist West and communist East to develop space technology. The most important race centred upon which side could reach the moon first.

Struggle meetings   Meetings in which opponents of the Chinese Communist regime were denounced, often by large crowds who shouted abuse at them. The targets were forced to confess their crimes and beg for forgiveness. Often they were beaten, sometimes even killed.

Triads   Chinese criminal organisation.

Xinjiang   A region in north-west China. The population is largely Muslim.

Key figures

Lin Biao (1907–71) An experienced soldier, Lin helped lead the Red Army to victory over the Japanese during the Second World War. Replaced Peng Duhaui as Minster of Defence in 1959. Helped build Mao's cult of personality by publishing the Little Red Book. After the Cultural Revolution he feared that Mao had turned against him and attempted to flee, dying when his plane crashed.

Chen Boda (1904–89) Mao's close ally and ideological adviser, Chen helped organise the CCP's propaganda. Editor of the Party's journal, *The Red Flag*. A radical, totally loyal to Mao and feared by other Communist leaders, he was accused of being a 'revisionist secret agent' and arrested.

Zhou Enlai (1898–1976) A long-time Communist, he travelled to Europe and helped found the CCP in France. Premier of the PRC from 1949. He was also foreign minister. Politically astute, he was careful never to alienate Mao. Genuinely popular, his death caused an outpouring of popular grief that led to demonstrations against radicals in the so-called 'Tiananmen Square Incident'.

Lei Feng (1940–62) A Chinese soldier who was committed to communism. After his death his devotion to communism was used to inspire other people to be loyal to the Party.

Chiang Kai-Shek (1887–1975) Chinese Nationalist leader who led the Kuomintang army against the Communists during the Civil War. When he was defeated, he was forced to flee to Taiwan, where he established a pro-Western government that was a capitalist ally of the West.

Nikita Khrushchev (1894–1971) Leader of the Soviet Union, he reduced the use of secret police terror used to control the Soviet people. Attempted to 'peacefully coexist' with the United States during the Cold War. Denounced Stalin's cult of personality in the so-called Secret Speech in 1956. This angered Mao, who believed that Khrushchev was not genuinely ideologically committed to communism. Forced out of office by the debacle of the Cuban Missile Crisis.

Dalai Lama (1935–) Tibetan Buddhist leader. When the PLA seized Tibet in 1951 he was forced to sign an agreement that gave power over Tibet to the Communist government. When Tibetans revolted against Chinese rule in 1959, he escaped into exile.

Ding Ling (1904–1986) Communist author who was imprisoned by the Kuomintang. Wrote critically about the failure of Party leaders to live up to their promises to create genuine gender equality. She was later damned as a 'rightist' and her work was banned. Imprisoned during the Cultural Revolution, she was sent to do manual labour on a farm before her release in 1978.

Jiang Qing (1914–91) Mao's fourth wife, she stayed out of politics until 1938 when Mao gave her the task of remoulding Chinese culture as part of the Cultural Revolution. A radical, she was a member of the so-called Gang of Four. Arrested after Mao's death, she was then imprisoned. She committed suicide in 1991.

Song Qingling (1893–1981) Second wife of Sun Yat-Sen, a leader of the 1911 Revolution that had helped end the rule of dynasties and created the Chinese republic. She was held in high esteem by Communist leaders and became the Vice-President of China. She travelled abroad to represent the PRC. Attacked during the Cultural Revolution, Zhou Enlai protected her from the Red Guards.

Liu Shaoqi (1898–1969) A long-time ally of Mao, as a student Liu had travelled to Moscow to study communism. Vice-Chairman of the CCP and named President of the PRC in 1959. A pragmatist, he angered Mao because he introduced rational, successful policies after the failure of the Great Leap Forward. A jealous Mao used the Cultural Revolution to attack Liu. He was stripped of his offices, tortured and imprisoned, dying due to of medical neglect in 1969.

Kang Sheng (1898–75) Trained in torture techniques by Stalin's secret police, Kang helped Mao persecute, torture and murder his opponents during the Cultural Revolution. Died of cancer in 1975.

Mao Zedong (1893–1976) Led the Communists to victory in the Civil War and established the PRC in 1949. Believed that China could only make up for its backward status by 'mobilising' the population into working to create a Communist state. Launched the Great Leap Forward in 1958 in an attempt to radically stimulate the economy. Ill-conceived, it led to a devastating famine. He was sidelined from politics but returned by launching the Cultural Revolution in 1965 that caused violence and chaos across China.

Timeline

1949   The formation of the PRC

1950   Campaign to Suppress Counter-Revolutionaries launched

Agrarian Reform Law

New Marriage Law

PLA begins reunification campaigns

China enters the Korean War in support of the Communist North against the United Nations

1951   'Resist America, Aid Korea' campaign begins

Launch of Three-Antis campaign

1952   Launch of Five-Antis campaign

1953   First Five-Year Plan for industry begins

1954   PRC's first constitution introduced

1957   The Hundred Flowers campaign

The Anti-Rightist campaign

1958   The Great Leap Forward begins

The First Peoples' Communes are formed

1959   Soviet advisers are withdrawn from China

Tibetan revolt is suppressed by the PLA

1962   'Little Red Book' published

1965   Yao Wenyuan publishes article that criticises Wu Han's play *Hai Rui Dismissed from Office*

The barefoot doctors are sent out on a large scale for the first time

1966   Cultural Revolution Group formed

Mao re-emerges into public view, swimming in the Yangtze River

Mao calls for a 'Cultural Revolution' and millions of Red Guards travel to Beijing to attend rallies in praise of him

1967   The 'January Storm'

'February Adverse Current'

1968   Liu Shaoqi officially removed from his post as Head of State

1969   Ninth Party Congress officially declares the Cultural Revolution to be over

Liu Shaoqi dies

1971   Lin Biao dies

1976   Zhou Enlai dies

Mao Zedong dies

The 'Gang of Four' are arrested and imprisoned

Mark scheme

Paper 2 requires two mark schemes, one for the AO2 assessments in Section A and another for Section B's AO1 assessment.

AO1 mark scheme: REVISED

- **Analytical focus**
- **Accurate detail**
- **Supported judgement**
- **Argument and structure**

Level	Marks	Description
1	1–3	• Simplistic statements. • Very limited accurate and relevant knowledge. • There is either no overall judgement, or it is very basic. • **Very little structure or argument.**
2	4–7	• Descriptive statements about key features. • Mostly accurate and relevant knowledge, but limited in terms of range and depth. • An overall judgement is presented, but with limited support. The judgement lacks clear criteria. • **The work shows the beginnings of structure and a limited attempt to create an argument.**
3	8–12	• Some analysis of key features. • Mostly accurate and relevant knowledge, used in a way that shows some understanding of the question. The range and depth may be limited in places. • An overall judgement is presented. It is supported with an attempt to establish criteria. • **Some structure and a generally clear argument.**
4	13–16	• Analysis of key features. • Sufficient accurate and relevant knowledge is used to answer most aspects of the question. • An overall judgement is presented. It is based on valid criteria, but may only be partially supported. • **A well-structured essay with a clear argument, although in places the argument may lack precision.**
5	17–20	• Sustained analysis of key features. • Sufficient accurate and relevant knowledge is used to answer all key aspects of the question. • An overall judgement is presented. It is based on valid criteria and is fully supported. The relative significance of the criteria may be considered while reaching the judgement. • **A well-structured essay with a clear argument which is communicated with precision.**

AO2 mark scheme:

- Analytical focus
- Accurate detail
- Supported judgement

Level	Marks	Description
1	1–3	• Surface-level comprehension of the sources, demonstrated by quoting or paraphrasing, without analysis. • Some relevant knowledge of the historical context is included, but links to the sources are limited. • There either no overall evaluation of the sources. Discussion of reliability and utility is very basic.
2	4–7	• Some understanding of the sources, demonstrated by selecting and summarising relevant information. • Some relevant knowledge of the historical context is linked to the extracts to support or challenge the detail they include. • An overall judgement is presented, but with limited support. Discussion of reliability and utility is based on a limited discussion of provenance and may reflect invalid assumptions.
3	8–12	• Understanding of the sources, demonstrated by some analysis of key points, explaining their meaning and valid inferences. • Relevant knowledge of the historical context is used to support inferences. Contextual knowledge is also used to expand on, support or challenge matters of detail. • An overall judgement is presented, which relates to the nature and purpose of the sources. The judgement is based on valid criteria, but the support is likely to be limited.
4	13–16	• Analysis of the sources, demonstrated by examining their evidence to make reasoned inferences. Valid distinctions are made between information and opinion. Treatment of the two sources may be uneven. • Relevant knowledge of the historical context is used to reveal and discuss the limitations of sources' content. The answer attempts to interpret the source material in the context of the values and assumptions of the society it comes from. • An overall judgement regarding the interpretation is presented which is supported by valid criteria. Evaluation of the sources reflects how much weight the evidence of the sources can bear. Aspects of the judgement may have limited support.
5	17–20	• Confident interrogation of both sources demonstrated by reasoned inferences. The answer shows a range of ways the sources can be used, making valid distinctions between information and opinion. • Relevant knowledge of the historical context is used to reveal and discuss the limitations of the sources' content. The answer interprets the source material in the context of the values and assumptions of the society it comes from. • An overall judgement regarding the interpretation is presented which is supported by valid criteria. Evaluation of the sources reflects how much weight the evidence of the sources can bear and may distinguish between the degrees to which aspects of the sources can be useful.

Answers

Page 7, Identify an argument

Sample 2 contains the argument.

Page 9, Spot the mistake

The paragraph does not get into the top level because although the factual detail contained in it is correct, it fails to make an explicit judgement on how successful land reform was and therefore does not sufficiently answer the question.

Page 11, Delete as applicable

The Communist Party had established political control in China between 1949 and 1954 to a **very great** extent. Although the Chinese People's Political Consultative Conference (CPPCC) was the main legislative body and initially included non-Communists, in fact the Communist Party and its Politburo held power. The CPPCC acted as a 'rubber stamp' to the wishes of the Politburo, allowing the Party to introduce its policies. Control of the government meant that the Communists could organise the country to ensure it could **definitely** establish complete control of China by splitting it into Bureaux and appointing loyal communists to key roles running each one. The part played by the PLA was **absolutely vital** to the establishment of control because it meant that opposition could be easily crushed. Party cadres enforced Communist policies in schools, factories, the civil service and the legal system. Democratic centralism gave the appearance of democratic representation but there was never any chance for voters to elect a different political party.

Page 13, RAG – Rate the timeline

1949	**October: Establishment of People's Republic of China.**
	December: Chiang Kai-Shek forced to retreat to Taiwan
1950	**April: Marriage Law announced**
	June: Korean War begins
	June: Land reform campaign begins in rural China
	October: PLA moves into Tibet
	November: China enters the Korean War against United Nations forces.
1951	**February: Resist America-Aid Korea campaign launched**
	April: The 17 point agreement between Tibet and China is signed
1951–2	**August–July: Three-Anti Campaign**
1952	**February–May: Five-Anti Campaign**
1953	**February: Beginning of Mutual Aid Teams is announced**
	July: Truce is signed between North and South Korea
1954	**September: China's first Constitution introduced**

Page 13, Develop the detail

Terror and violence were very significant factors in the establishment of Communist control in China in the period 1949–53. For example, the Three and Five Antis campaigns removed many opponents. **For example, corrupt officials and well-off business owners were targeted.** This was popular with some people **because it appeared to show that the government was serious in trying to make Chinese society more equal.** It showed that the Communists would remove their enemies **and this meant that potential opponents of the regime were intimidated into passive acceptance.** The campaigns were boosted by the Korean War because the new government could use the war as an excuse. **They could lock up or force into exile anyone that they believed was not ideologically committed enough, using the excuse that they were traitors working for China's enemies during the war.** It was not just terror and violence that helped establish Communist control. Some Communist policies were popular with many Chinese people. **For example, the land reform programme was very popular,** particularly among the poorest peasants. After years of being repressed by greedy landlords, they now had the opportunity to own their own land. Despite this, terror and violence were very significant because they spread fear and intimidated opponents into submission.

Page 25, Spot the inference

Land reform benefited the peasants economically. **(Inference)**

Poorer peasants took advantage of the land reform programme to exploit landlords. **(Summarise)**

The land reform programme turned the peasants into ideologically committed Communists. **(Cannot be justified from the source)**

The peasants kept on demanding money and food from the landlords until finally they gave them everything. This greatly improved the life of the peasants. **(Paraphrase)**

Page 27, RAG – Rate the timeline

1950	Agrarian Reform Law introduced
	New Marriage Law announced
	The Korean War begins
1951	'Resist America–Aid Korea' campaign begins
	Foreigners are expelled from China
	Three-Antis Campaign
1952	Five-Antis Campaign
1953	Truce signed between North and South Korea
	Soviet dictator Joseph Stalin dies and is replaced by Nikita Khrushchev
	Plans to introduce Mutual Aid Teams announced
	First Five-Year Plan for industry begins
1954	China's first constitution introduced
1955	Membership in Agricultural Producers Cooperatives reaches 41 per cent of peasant farmers
1956	December Almost 88 per cent of peasant farmers in higher-level Agricultural Producers Co-operatives
	Co-operatives reaches 96 per cent of peasant farmers
	Hundred Flowers Campaign launched
1957	Soviet Union launches first satellite, Sputnik, into orbit

Page 31, Complete the paragraph

There is no doubt that the weather contributed to the Great Famine. Party cadres, hoping to advance their careers, lied to Mao about how high food production was, leading him to set targets that were totally unrealistic. However, it was Mao who wrongly believed that mass mobilisation could overcome the limitations of China's economy. It was Mao who personally intervened to accelerate the creation of the communes. It was Mao's use of terror previously that intimidated the Party cadres and thus kept them from telling him the truth about the reality of the famine. Therefore, it was Mao's policies that were responsible for the Great Famine to a very large extent.

Page 31, Explain the difference

Source 1 is a piece of Communist propaganda and provides a very positive evaluation of the communes because it is from an official Communist Party publication that has a political vested interest in spreading the idea the that the communes were successful and popular. In contrast, Source 2 provides a more valuable and truthful analysis of the reality of the communes. It was never meant for public attention, but rather to help Communist Party leaders to understand exactly what was happening in the country.

Page 33, The flaw in the argument

This argument fails to provide a balanced argument. Although the factual material here is mostly correct, it fails to address the fact that the success of the plan came at the cost of the personal freedoms of the workers. They did have more stable jobs, but they were totally controlled by the Communist Party. In fact, the plan focused on stimulating heavy industry and there were very few consumer goods in the shops.

Page 39, Explain the difference

The difference between the sources can be explained by the different motives of the authors. The author of Source 1 is writing in the hope of ending the Great Leap Forward. At this time, Peng travelled to his home village and talked to the peasants. Therefore, he has a very realistic and factually correct view of the impact of Mao's economic policies. In contrast, Mao is seeking to defend the Great Leap Forward. He was compelled to do this because he was personally responsible for introducing the Great Leap and if he admitted that the policy had failed, he would be open to criticism. This is why Mao stresses the positive successes of the policy and refuses to recognise how much of a failure it was.

Page 55, RAG – Rate the timeline

1964:	PLA first collects Mao's quotations and publishes them in the Little Red Book. Lin Biao, head of the PLA writes the foreword to the book.
1966:	
August:	Mao displays his own 'Big Character Poster' urging the people to 'Bombard the Headquarters.'
	PLA help transport millions of young Red Guards to rallies led by Mao in Beijing.
	Universities and middle-schools across China closed down.
	Red Guards, mainly students, launch campaign against the Four Olds
November:	Radical factory and office workers form their own Red Guard units.
December:	Rival Red Guard factions battle in Shanghai.
1967:	
January:	Radicals in Shanghai overthrow party leadership in the city and set up a Commune.
February:	'February Adverse Current': Politburo criticises excesses of the Cultural Revolution and PLA launches attack on radicals to suppress Red Guard violence.
	Liu and Deng placed under house arrest.
	Liu subjected to struggle meetings.
	Peng Duhuai beaten and tortured.
	Middle-schools reopen.
August:	Mao declares the purging of capitalist roaders in the PLA to be 'un-strategic.'
1968:	Liu Shaoqi expelled from the CCP.
	'Up to the mountains and down to the villages' campaign and Barefoot Doctors campaigns begin.
	PLA sent into Shaanxi and Guangxi provinces to stop civil war. 'PLA launches 'cleansing of class ranks' campaign which arrests 1.8 million people.
	Universities reopen.
1969:	Lin Biao named as Mao's successor.
	Deng sent to Jiangxi province to live as a regular worker.
	Liu Shaoqi dies in prison.
1971:	Lin Biao dies in a plane crash
1972:	United States President Richard Nixon visits China.
1973–4:	Anti-Confucius campaign.
	Peng Dehuai dies in prison
1975:	Death of Chiang Kai-Shek;
	New Chinese constitution makes Mao Zedong Thought the guiding principle of the CCP.
1976:	
January	Death of Zhou Enlai
April	The Tiananmen Incident
September	Death of Mao
October	Arrest of the Gang of Four.

Page 61, Spot the mistake

This paragraph does not get into Level 5 because the judgement is too simplistic. It fails to show an awareness that legal equality did not in fact guarantee that women were treated equally. Traditional attitudes to gender equality were much harder to change than the law.

Page 63, Spot the mistake

This paragraph does not get into Level 5 because although the factual detail is accurate, it does not contain an explicit link back to the question. It lists ways that the lives of women changed, but does not include a judgement on how far life actually improved or not.

Page 63, Eliminate irrelevance

Some progress had been made towards legal gender equality by 1976. The 1950 Marriage Law made men and women legally equal partners in marriage, made divorce rights legal and prevented arranged marriages. Mao had long talked about how much he wanted to create legal authority. ~~In 1913 he had written about his dislike of arranged marriages, calling them a form of slavery. He had himself had a marriage arranged by his family, though he never considered the bride to be his true wife.~~ However, despite the 1950 Marriage Law, in traditional rural communities this legal authority did not always mean that women were treated equally. Traditional views of women as subservient remained, despite the efforts of the Women's Association, whose representatives were sent to the countryside to educate the peasants. The least progress was made in Islamic areas like Xinjiang. Here, arranged marriages were an important custom and continued regardless of legal changes. During the Cultural Revolution some young women became Red Guards, giving them status, authority and respect that they had not previously had.

Page 65, You're the examiner

Level: 4

Reasons for choosing this level: This answer starts with a clear judgement that explicitly answers the question, and provides specific factual detail, including statistical evidence, to answer the question. However, it lacks a concluding analytical link back to the question at the end of the paragraph to show how the evidence proves that education did not improve and it does not apply the evidence to make a judgement of how the level of educational improvement changes across the date range. This is a must for a question that focuses on the entire date range of the course.

Page 65, Complete the paragraph

The government carried out several reforms to the system of education. Primary schools were established throughout the country, along with courses for adult education. These reforms aimed at improving national standards of literacy. The brightest children were given an advanced education by the best teachers. During the Cultural Revolution, education in China collapsed as schools and universities closed for two years.

Overall, therefore, **although some improvements were made, particularly for younger students, the government failed to improve education because access to the best education was still unequal and at the end of period schools and universities were closed and many young people were not educated at all.**

Page 67, Delete as applicable

The Communist government's reforms had a **limited** impact on the health of the Chinese people between these dates. The reforms did help educate the Chinese people to help prevent the spread of disease. Patriotic Health Movements taught them to prevent the spread of disease. They were taught to stop using human waste as fertiliser and to dig deep wells to collect water. Posters taught them how to catch vermin and to drain the swamps that bred the mosquitoes that spread malaria. The Women's Association played a key role in improving the standard of maternity care for women, reducing the risk of childbirth and lowering the infant mortality rate. However, what modern hospitals that there were helped only the people in the big cities. Rural peasant communities had only basic clinics. Many peasants still relied on traditional Chinese herbal medicine. The government only spent a tiny amount of money on health care, so the policies had to focus mainly on prevention rather than actual treatment. Clearly, the government reforms had a **limited** impact on the health of the Chinese people.

Page 69, Delete as applicable

Jiang Qing did replace old Chinese art and culture with one based on Communism to a **partial** extent. She attacked traditional theatre and opera as 'bourgeois' and 'revisionist'. Performances that included 'old-fashioned' ideas such as romance, religion or ancestor worship were banned or rewritten. Directors, composers and writers who defended traditional performances, literature and art were blacklisted or imprisoned. Some were attacked by the Red Guards and others committed suicide to escape the threats and violence. Temples and religious monuments were destroyed, foreign books were destroyed and all foreign plays were banned. However, many peasants were unaffected. Furthermore, old ideas such as ancestor worship were not destroyed: when Zhou Enlai died there was a spontaneous outpouring of grief during the Qingming festival, the traditional time to honour respected ancestors. Therefore, it would be accurate to say that Jiang Qing succeeded only to a **partial** extent in the sense that

Page 71, Identify the concept

'Communist policies had little impact on Chinese culture in the period 1965–76.' How far do you agree with this statement? **(Consequence)**

How far did Communist policies towards culture change in the period 1949–76? **(Change/ continuity)**

How accurate is it to say that the growth in influence of Jiang Qing was the most important consequence of Communist policies towards culture, 1965–76? **(Significance)**

To what extent was Mao's decision to launch the Cultural Revolution caused by his desire to re-mould Chinese culture? **(Cause)**

How far do you agree that the reasons for the launching of the Hundred Flowers campaign and the Cultural Revolution were the same? **(Similarity/difference)**

Page 73, Explain the difference

Source 1 is very different from Source 1 because it is an official government document. It sets out the legal guidelines for the treatment of religious believers. The government would be very concerned to portray itself as tolerant to both its own people and, vitally, foreign observers who would have been worried by the treatment of religious believers by the Communists. The Communists had won support during the Civil War in part because they promised to make China a fairer and more equal society, and this constitution was written to help the government portray itself as one that would improve the rights of the Chinese people. The second source is different because it provides an insight into the reality of the way the government treated religious believers. As an eyewitness account, it provides first-hand personal testimony of the failure of the government to live up to the promises made in Source 1.

Page 75, Explain the difference

Source 1 is very different from Source 2 because it is written by a close adviser of Mao who had regular personal contact with him. As a result, it provides a private perspective, revealing Mao's intimate thoughts about his family. The details of the scene described would not have been made public. It reveals that despite his belief in Communist ideology that was strongly opposed to religion, he still had sympathy for the supportive role that religious belief could offer the people in times of hardship. In contrast, Source 2 shows the results of the public policy of the Communists: it shows how much the Communists repressed believers in Christianity. The source is also different because it is written by a victim of the terror, rather than a colleague of Mao's. While Source 1 describes Mao's attitudes to traditional Chinese beliefs, the author in Source 2 is a Catholic, a faith that the Communists saw as linked to the imperialist West. Therefore, the attitude is much harsher.